The Mindful Leader

This book is dedicated to David Wilkinson
(Principal, St John's College, Durham) and
Jeff Greenman (President, Regent College, Vancouver).
Both of these leaders are exemplars of mindful, caring and
decisive leadership through demanding times.

The Mindful Leader
Embodying Christian Wisdom

Peter Shaw

CANTERBURY
PRESS

First published in 2018 by the Canterbury Press Norwich
Editorial office
3rd Floor, Invicta House
108–114 Golden Lane
London EC1Y 0TG, UK

Canterbury Press is an imprint of Hymns Ancient & Modern Ltd
(a registered charity)
13A Hellesdon Park Road, Norwich,
Norfolk NR6 5DR, UK

www.canterburypress.co.uk

British Library Cataloguing in Publication data

A catalogue record for this book is available
from the British Library

978 1 78622 113 1

Typeset by Rebecca Goldsmith

Printed and bound in Great Britain by
CPI Group (UK) Croydon

Contents

Foreword

Leadership comes in many forms. We probably all have our own favourite leaders from across history but what distinguishes one from another? What makes a 'Mindful Leader'?

Leadership values are as important as leadership skills and our values are established from the very start of our lives through our childhood experiences, our education and our early careers. The skill of leadership includes the ability to operate with clear values and to be deliberate about the sources of wisdom we draw from.

As we all reflect on the issues that modern political, business and educational leaders are currently addressing, the need for a strong set of values has never been stronger and I am delighted Peter Shaw has turned his attention to presenting the Christian narrative to the subject of being a mindful leader. His expertise as a senior manager, a coach and an outstanding leader who draws on his Christian understanding puts him in a unique position to offer practical guidance founded on a strong theological base.

Over the last 20 years I have been leading teams in the corporate, charity and public sector in such diverse organizations as Kingfisher, Sainsbury's, HMV, Cancer Research UK and UK Research and Innovation. In parallel I have been helping to lead my local church and Cathedral and simultaneously trying to provide my children with the values that will underpin their lives. The leadership challenges across different areas are, in my view, the same and the Christian wisdom set out by Peter provides a compelling framework.

Leadership requires the use of our heart, our head and our

hands – balancing the contribution from each one to the circumstances. As I have taken on bigger, more challenging, leadership roles the support of strong teams has been incredibly important to me and I have spent more time thinking through the way to engage the hearts and heads of people. As Peter sets out in this book mindful leadership provides a framework within which teams can grow underpinned by a Christian understanding.

Across the different organizations where I have been involved there have been many different approaches to leadership. This may have been driven by different values of the various leaders or by different operating circumstances. What I have observed though is that people are genuinely interested in the way a Christian understands and approaches leadership – and it has been a great opportunity to demonstrate how the values set out thousands of years ago apply just as much to today's society.

As a leader one of my greatest pleasures is seeing how individuals within my teams have grown in confidence and become the next generation of leaders. They have learned to manage and motivate others and have been able to embrace increased responsibility based on their own set of values and they are having to address many of the questions that Peter poses though the book.

I strongly commend this book to any leader or aspiring leader. It is a book that will continually ask questions of leaders and will, I hope, equip us all to consider how we might apply Christian wisdom in a thoughtful and sensitive way, whether or not we come with a faith perspective.

Ian Kenyon

Chief Finance Officer and Deputy Chief Executive

United Kingdom Research and Innovation (UKRI)

Introduction

It has been a privilege to work as a coach with senior leaders who bring a wide range of different world views. It has been a delight to engage with leaders who describe themselves as Muslim, Hindu, Sikh, Christian, Jewish, Buddhist, Humanist, Atheist, and Agnostic. Each one has applied the values that are precious to them, shaped by their religious or secular tradition and perspective.

Some of the most interesting organizations I have worked with have been global organizations where there has been a healthy interplay of ideas with leaders bringing different perspectives shaped by their cultural and faith backgrounds. It is always helpful to reflect on what has shaped a leader's perspective about what is most important in leading well, and to ponder what can be learnt from others who have a different heritage and world view.

The key influences on me began with growing up in Methodism in the 1950s and early 1960s with its focus on the hard work of applying Christian faith and understanding. When I was studying at Durham University the combination of the traditional worship in the college chapel and engagement with the contemporary approach of the University Christian Union made me think about the relevance of Christian thinking to academic learning and the type of work I might be equipped to do.

Studying at a trans-denominational college in Vancouver brought into sharp focus the interrelationship between theology and business issues. Working for 32 years in the UK Government taught me the importance of integrity, thoroughness, fair mind-

1

edness and rigorous analysis. The last sixteen years working as a coach with executive leaders and teams across six continents has helped me focus on the value of interrelating insights from different faith perspectives into the attitudes and approaches of leaders and managers, irrespective of their sector or geography.

In recent years I have had the opportunity to work with post-graduate students from across the world at universities and colleges in the UK and Canada. My objective is to enable students of whatever age to understand more clearly how their faith and cultural backgrounds affect their thinking and can provide them with a valuable frame of reference when making leadership decisions. I also seek to encourage them to keep learning from the insights of those who come from different perspectives.

The focus on mindfulness in recent years has drawn from the rich insights of the Buddhist faith. I have worked with Buddhist and Hindu leaders who bring a calmness and gentleness which has equipped them to bring a distinctive, inclusive and effective leadership approach. Leaders who have faith or no faith are learning from this focus of being mindful of yourself and others.

This book seeks to draw on the themes that are at the heart of the Christian Gospel with my intent being to draw out the relevance of these themes for leaders and managers. Many of these themes also feature in other faith traditions which is perhaps why leaders who come from different faith traditions can often work well together. I am equally conscious that sometimes people from different faith traditions can sometimes find it difficult to work together because of an apparent unwillingness to learn from those who come from a different and equally strongly held viewpoint.

My intent for those readers who are unsure or sceptical about the relevance of Christian understanding to leadership is to encourage them to see the relevance and coherence of Christian principles to leading well. In the same way that mindfulness has provided a rich stream of insights for leaders and managers I hope that this book will demonstrate that a Christian perspective brings a wealth of wisdom that overlaps and complements insights from mindfulness drawn from the Buddhist and Hindu traditions.

My intent for those readers who bring a Christian perspective is to equip them to apply Christian wisdom in a thoughtful and sensitive way, engaging in partnership with those who come from different perspectives.

I have divided the book into three main sections which focus on our heart, our head and our hands. Under each section I explore eight themes. The themes are evidenced from the Old and the New Testaments thereby identifying them as part of the Judeo-Christian tradition. Each chapter includes a case-study and some questions for reflection either individually or in a group.

In Part 1 on the Heart I start with the focus on new life and resurrection and consider forgiveness, love, gentleness, reconciliation, vulnerability, hope and joy. In Part 2 on the Head I explore truth, crucifixion, healing, humility, freedom, judgement, peace and self-control. In Part 3 on Hands I look at the practical application of the themes explored under the heart and head through exploring; responsibility, sacrifice, community, communion, faithfulness, perseverance, kindness and patience. In Part 4 I look at how we can embody in our leadership these three different themes and key questions we might ask ourselves about applying our heart, head and hands. There are other themes such as redemption that are not explored in this book and are worthy of a separate study.

I debated whether to use as the subtitle to the book 'embodying

Christian wisdom ' or 'embodying Christian insights'. It could be either. Solomon asked for wisdom above all else. Perhaps what I am seeking to do is to draw insights for those in very varied leadership roles from the wealth of wisdom embedded in the Judeo-Christian understanding of life in all its richness and complexity.

This book is not intended to be a definitive and exclusive work. My intent is to set you thinking and to enable you to explore the relevance of some of these themes for the way you lead and manage whatever type of organization you are in and whatever part of the world you based in. My Christian faith and understanding underpins my approach to enabling those who have leadership responsibilities to exercise these with confidence, clarity and compassion. In my coaching work with senior leaders across six continents I am convinced that the themes set out in the book are highly pertinent for many leaders in a fast-changing world.

It is my hope that this book will be relevant to thoughtful leaders of any faith or no faith, as well as relevant to Christians in, or aspiring to be in, leadership roles. To those sceptics about the relevance of a faith perspective I hope it will give you some useful insights alongside other sources of perspective and learning. For those who come with a faith perspective I hope it will give you confidence that eternal truths about engaging and leading well continue to be highly pertinent to leading and managing in the twenty-first century.

Canon Professor Peter Shaw
Godalming, Surrey

PART ONE

Heart

At the centre of Christian understanding is the belief in restoration, new life and resurrection. This section starts with the central theme of resurrection and then explores a sequence of areas where the attitude of the heart is central. We look in turn at resurrection, forgiveness, love, gentleness, reconciliation, vulnerability, hope and joy.

These themes encapsulate an attitude of mind that believes renewal and new life is possible with forgiveness, love and gentleness leading to reconciliation. It assumes that the acknowledgement of vulnerability is a starting point for a sense of hope whatever the current reality, with the prospect of an underlying sense of joy, however tough the circumstances.

1

Resurrection

I recently visited a part of London I had not been to for a few years. What had been a shabby area of 1960s offices was now transformed into an attractive office development conducive to modern ways of working. The place had new life and energy. As I walked around some of the offices there was a buzz with lots of conversations in an environment where people were encouraged to be engaging purposefully with each other.

I visited a prison recently where the Executive Team were talking about lives transformed through the education programme and through the opportunities to do meaningful work in the community. People's lives, which had previously seemed hopeless, had now got new energy and purpose, with a growing sense that there could be a meaningful and fulfilling life after prison.

I recently talked with a 50 year old who is doing an interim HR senior manager role. A few years ago she had felt bogged down and resentful that she had not been promoted. There was a reluctance in her to take on responsibility and a tendency to blame others for her lack of success. There had been a breakthrough: one of her bosses had helped her realize that she had potential to do bigger roles and that it was her own self-limiting beliefs that were holding her back.

She needed to break out of the chrysalis that stopped her from taking on assignments that would develop her confidence and reputation. She decided she needed to come out of the shadows and take a grip on her own contribution. This new attitude helped renew her energy and gave her the motivation to see projects through to a successful completion. She was transformed from being timid and defensive into being open and positive.

The good leader can spot the potential for new life and energy in most situations. When the leader brings energy, hope and a sense of the future there can be a knock-on transformative effect with new life and growth springing up. As soon as there is a momentum in the right direction people are attracted to an enterprise where there is energy and hope: they want to be part of success and forward movement.

New life is infectious as people are attracted to being part of an adventure that is forward-moving. Equally when a venture is struggling and there is little sense of new life or hope the natural inclination is to want to 'jump ship' and not be part of a slow death.

New life and resurrection is a constant theme in the Christian Gospel. Transformation and new life is integral to the Christian message of renewal and hope. The resurrection of Jesus after his crucifixion is seen as Jesus overcoming death and breaking the notion that life always ends in death and despair. The experience of the resurrection transformed the disciples from beaten and dispirited followers at the crucifixion, into apostles willing to go to prison and die for their faith. They became witnesses of Jesus' resurrection bringing good news of hope about transformed lives. Paul talks about the power of the resurrection flowing from participating in the suffering of others. Peter writes about the living hope that flows from the resurrection of Jesus Christ from the dead and the resulting inheritance that can never perish, spoil or fade.

Perhaps the biggest insight from the Christian understanding of human nature and the world in which we live is this emphasis on the scope for new life, transformation and resurrection. This firm belief in new life and resurrection means that no situation is regarded as irredeemable and no person need be completely overwhelmed by fear. The belief in new life gives leaders the rationale to seek to inspire people to give of their best and to develop their confidence and capabilities in a way they had not previously thought possible.

Sometimes the seed has to die for there to be new life. Sometimes the old branches have to be cut off in order to let the new shoots grow. Allowing for new life and resurrection is not without pain. It does require decisive action which can look painful but, as every parent knows, allowing a child to grow into adulthood requires letting go. Life only grows to fullness when the parent allows any desire they may have to control to die, so that young life can fully blossom into adulthood embracing freedom alongside a clear sense of responsibility.

New life needs careful nurturing. The transformed building or the reformed life requires the investment of time and energy. There needs to be commitment to the hard work of transformation, alongside moments of revelation when someone takes a step-change in confidence and begins to blossom, becoming the leader they always had the potential to become.

Amanda felt bogged down in her work. There was a perfectionism which kept her trying to refine a piece of work long after its due deadline. There was a negativity about her approach which meant that she focused on the downsides of any approach. There was a defensiveness about her manner which meant that colleagues rarely shared their ideas with her. There was a frustration in her face which meant that nobody particularly wanted to spend time with her or encourage her.

Amanda's new boss could see that she had potential. He observed the flashes of insight and the sparkle that could sometimes appear in her eyes. Her boss teamed her up with a mentor who was a great encourager, and a coach with a brief to help her recognize her capabilities. The mentor helped her look forward in a more positive and decisive way. The coach helped Amanda recognize that her self-perception was getting in the way of the new energy and life which was latent within her.

Amanda's coach helped her face into the reality of how she was projecting herself. He helped Amanda to believe that she could change her approach and be transformed in her impact. Amanda felt a growing sense of new life in herself. Her positive approach was noticed and she was given more opportunities. The negative internal forces holding her back were being held at bay. It was as if she was a new person transformed in her mind-set and approach to the future. She was witness to the transformation that can happen. It felt as if part of her had been resurrected from a slow meandering death.

For reflection

- What is the hope for the future that is in you that could lead to new life and transformation?
- What attitudes have to die and be left behind before your attitudes and approach can be transformed?
- Who are the people who can best help you to leave the negative behind and embrace new possibilities and new life with conviction?
- Which parts of your attitude of mind need to be resurrected from the grip of your inner demons?

2

Forgiveness

How often do you forgive someone who has let you down? Does there need to be a sense of remorse before you readily forgive? Do you forgive someone even though you have little confidence that they will alter their approach? When someone's behaviour is having an adverse effect on others who is the neighbour who you particularly want to support? If you forgive someone and they do not change their behaviour the detrimental effect on others could go on indefinitely.

There may be a difference between forgiveness within a family and forgiveness within a work context. Forgiveness within a family might be never-ending because of the bonds of love that keep a family together. Forgiveness within a work or wider community context may well need boundaries, for repeated forgiveness can have a detrimental effect on others towards whom you also have a responsibility.

The ability to forgive and move on and not bear grudges is important for any leader. The risk of not forgiving is that you end up carrying the baggage of resentment. Forgiveness is important both for the receiver in order to have a new start, and for the giver in terms of their moving on, and being open to a fresh start in the relationship with the individual concerned.

In the Old Testament forgiveness is linked to a God of grace who is ready to forgive. Deuteronomy says that mercy and forgiveness belong to God. The Old Testament understanding of forgiveness is expressed clearly in Exodus in the words: the Lord is a compassionate and gracious God, slow to anger and abounding in love and faithfulness, maintaining love to thousands and forgiving wickedness, rebellion and sin.

Forgiveness is rooted in the nature of God as gracious, but His forgiveness is not indiscriminate. Penitence is seen as a prerequisite of forgiveness. The Psalmist talks about removing our transgressions from us as far as the east is from the west. Micah speaks of our iniquities being thrown into the depth of the sea. Such language emphasizes the completeness of forgiveness.

Within the New Testament some of the Greek words translated as forgiveness mean, 'to deal graciously with', 'to send away', 'to release', and 'a passing by'. The expectation in the New Testament is that the forgiven individual forgives others, as evidenced in the Lord's Prayer. The expectation is that forgiveness is wholehearted. In a number of parables Jesus insists on the demonstration of mercy and forgiveness. He places a strong emphasis on forgiving a brother or sister 'from your heart'.

The theme of forgiveness is central to the work of John the Baptist who preached the baptism of repentance for the forgiveness of sins. Peter's preaching links forgiveness and the receiving of the Holy Spirit. Faith and repentance are not thought of as merits that deserve receiving forgiveness: the focus is on forgiveness leading to receiving the grace of God.

There will be frequent occasions when you feel let down by others. Your natural inclination may be not to want to forgive them. You feel let down and find it difficult to think positively about the individual. Perhaps the key is to think into what was going on in their heart and mind which led to the words or actions that have caused you angst. This reflection might lead you into thinking through how you can influence their context or reaction so that they are able to respond more constructively going forward. Forgiving someone might be about dealing graciously with them, releasing yourself from the grip of disappointment or anger and moving on from a situation where you feel let down into seeking a constructive way of seeing possibilities going forward.

When you feel let down by someone it is worth reflecting on how you leave this sense of being let down behind and equip that person to be ready to cope more effectively with different situations going forward. There can be enormous satisfaction in mentoring someone to move on from what has been holding them back and seeing opportunities going forward.

Sometimes we need to forgive people for their behaviour while recognizing that they are unlikely to change. Once you have been adversely affected by someone's behaviour, you are rightly going to be cautious and prepared for when you might be treated unfairly or detrimentally again. Being utterly courteous and professional, while being wary, is a way of protecting yourself when you experience behaviours that are unfair and uncalled for.

There are times when the approach or behaviour of a colleague is so bad that justice trumps forgiveness. The abusing of individuals and treating them with distain needs to be addressed directly. Forgiveness might be relevant at a later date when there has been remorse. But when behaviour is clearly dangerous, quick decisive action is needed without hesitation.

Rachel felt unhappy about the way she had been treated within the firm where she worked. She experienced a macho culture where people were aggressive and argumentative in tone. She felt continually put down and unappreciated. At times it felt as if she was being bullied.

When there was an anonymized 360° feedback exercise Rachel included some direct comments about the management approach. Her comments must have been echoed by others because her manager initially went quiet and then for a period was apologetic about his manner. It was not long though before he reverted to his previous behaviour pattern of being aggressive at the mildest provocation.

Rachel was undecided about whether she wanted to forgive her boss. She sought to understand the pressures on him that had led to this type of behaviour. She kept her distance and was wary of his approach. She was conscious that there was a resentment inside her that she needed to deal with. On one occasion when her boss was clearly out of order with an aggressive comment she decided to speak to him about this behaviour within three days. She chose a moment when he appeared more relaxed and talked about her reaction to his comment.

Her boss recognized the concern in a way that surprised Rachel: he explained why some of the pressures on him had led to this type of reaction. They agreed that Rachel should feel free to say when her boss's behaviour felt unreasonable. At this point Rachel understood how she could handle her own frustrations and began to forgive her boss because he had begun to explain and apologize about his behaviour.

For reflection

- What attitude and approach does someone need to exhibit before you will readily forgive them?
- When might not forgiving someone lead to a build-up of resentment in you which is unhelpful?
- How best can you both forgive someone and be wary of them?
- What type of actions require firm action rather than forgiveness?

3

Love

To what extent is love relevant in the workplace? Unending love seems inconsistent with the discipline needed in the workplace. A love which is continually forgiving and is undemanding might seem like utopia for some and grossly unfair for others. Love that always says yes with no boundaries can be disruptive, leaving people unclear about where an organization is going and their position in the organization.

The benevolent employer might have a deep love for their workforce. They might be genuinely concerned about their livelihood and wellbeing, but the good employer cannot let the love for their staff blind them to the economic and political realities in which they operate.

Loving their staff is about embracing reality and not suppressing it. It involves giving hard messages, where tough love sits alongside kindness. It is unkind to keep pretending that someone is doing a good job when it is painfully obvious that there are deficiencies. If for example a teacher is not doing their job well it is not being kind to the teacher or the pupils to protect them from that reality. Loving the teacher involves helping them face into the reality of disinterested pupils and dissatisfied parents.

When you love a friend you spend time with them, listen to them, engage with them at a deep level and work together for a better future. When you allow yourself to be committed to the success of a colleague or member of your staff you are treasuring their insights and seeing their potential. You may not describe yourself as loving them but you are listening to them, engaging with them and helping them to move forward with a frame of mind that is balanced, wholesome and integrated.

Love often involves compassion so that, when someone is down or has been knocked, you enable them to rise up with new confidence and insight. You do not beat someone when they are down or take advantage of their weakness. You help them to take stock and to reflect so they are compassionate about themselves and nurture a new sense of hope in future possibilities.

The Old Testament is full of references to the practical outworking of an attitude of love. Daniel talks of a covenant of love. Joel talks of being slow to anger and abounding in love. Micah focuses on acting justly and loving mercy. The Psalmist talks of unfailing love, and of love and faithfulness meeting together. In one Psalm the phrase, 'His love endures ever' occurs twenty-six times.

Jesus urges his followers to love their enemies and pray for them. Jesus talks of the two greatest commandments with the first being to 'love the Lord your God with all your heart and with all your soul and with all your mind', and the second being to, 'love your neighbour as yourself'. Jesus urges his hearers not to neglect justice or the love of God. The Gospel writer John talks of loving one another and remaining in God's love, with true disciples being those who love one another.

Paul describes love as patient and kind, but he also talks about speaking the truth in love. He refers to love coming from the hope that is in his hearers. Paul encourages his readers to be at one in a loving, supporting relationship with a strong sense of self-sacrifice and mutual support.

The most telling part of Jesus' second commandment is to love your neighbour 'as yourself'. This involves exercising the same love in relation to others that you want to exercise in relation to yourself. It includes being unrelentingly supportive of others and not stopping loving them when they let you down. This might well mean giving them clear feedback. Bringing a sense of loving someone in the workplace is about not being a soft touch. It is about a depth of understanding, a clarity of perspective and a directness that is expressed in a fully supportive way.

The exercise of love in the workplace is best done in a way that is objective, rooted in proper and understood procedures and good governance, and is always backed up by evidence and on-going practical support. Love in the workplace is the exact opposite of emotional pressure. There is no intent to distort or manipulate behaviour or abuse positions of authority or influence.

Practical love is about enhancing the freedom of choice for individuals and not seeking to diminish it through authoritarian pressure or blinkered expectations or stiffly imposed behaviours. Agreed values which embed humility, mutual support and trust require honesty and transparency if they are to be sustained over the longer term.

As soon as the degree of support for someone begins to look manipulative or self-satisfying danger signals need to be raised. The risks of empathy and support turning into unreasonable emotional pressure are always there. If there is any hint of a strong sense of supportive love becoming tainted by a desire to control or to satisfy emotional self-interest, this needs to be faced up to as a risk and addressed.

In the workplace love that is patient and kind can be hugely liberating, enabling someone to find in themselves strength and potential they never thought existed. On the other hand the risk of empathetic love turning into manipulation and control needs to be faced up to honestly and decisively.

Ray had built up a strong team on the project he was leading and became very fond of different members of his team. He once described himself as adoring his team and was slightly taken aback when a colleague asked him what he meant by that description. The comment made him reflect on why he loved his team so much. He felt empathetic towards them as individuals and wanted them to grow and develop. He loved members of his team rather like the way he adored some of his nephews in the way they were growing up and developing into young adults.

Ray recognized the limits of this love. Like a good parent Ray needed to develop his team to the point where they would want to spin off and do other things. Love was about extending their horizons and not limiting their scope. Love was about encouraging them to fly free and not seeking to control their hopes and aspirations for the future. Practical love needed to be kindly and generous but it also included a degree of protection to help his team avoid making mistakes. This practical concern was about flagging up risks and not controlling decisions. For Ray the love from the leader was about equipping people to make good choices and never trying to control those choices.

For reflection

- When should love in the workplace be patient and kind, and when might directness be needed to protect people from themselves?
- How best do you show love and empathy for a colleague and be utterly professional in every part of the working relationship?
- What are the danger points for you when too much empathy for an individual can distort your judgement about their capabilities?
- How best do you ensure that your capacity to love and encourage others is recharged through the support of others and not drained through overuse?

4

Gentleness

Gentleness is the antithesis of many people's perception of the effective leader. Gentle can imply soft and weak, but the reality is that leaders who are confident and comfortable in themselves can be compassionate and gentle in their approach because they are not trying to demonstrate their strength all the time.

Gentleness is a key quality in some professions and areas of work, and is much underrated in other areas. The surgeon has to explore someone's anatomy carefully and gently before deciding where to use the scalpel. The architect is producing drawings with careful precision, gently and meticulously measuring out the lines, angles and elevations. The counsellor is gently probing someone's personal history in order to understand the nature of the interactions that have influenced that person's emotional wellbeing.

Within the Old Testament in the book of Proverbs the contrast is drawn between a gentle answer that turns away wrong and a harsh word that stirs up anger. The tongue of the wise is described as adorning knowledge while the mouth of the fool is described as gushing folly. In one of the later Proverbs Solomon says that through patience a ruler can be persuaded, and a gentle tongue can break a bone. Gentleness is seen as a way of winning someone's confidence and not as a sign of weakness.

Jesus describes himself as gentle and humble in heart. He invites those who are weary and burdened to learn from him and find rest for their souls because of his gentleness. He says, 'My yoke is easy, my burden is light'.

The theme of gentleness is taken up in the Epistles. Galatians lists gentleness as one of the fruits of the Spirit. The Ephesians are encouraged to be gentle. When Paul writes to Timothy he describes the qualifications for overseers and deacons being that they are temperate and hospitable, not violent but gentle, not awesome and not a lover of money. Paul writing to the Corinthians talks of his forthcoming visit to the Corinthians. He asks whether they would prefer him to come with a rod of discipline or in love with a gentle spirit. The apostle Peter in describing the relationship between wives and husbands talks about respect and the unfading beauty of a gentle and quiet spirit.

Gentleness is not straightforward and is rarely the easy option. Gentleness requires calmness, care and consideration which may not always come as easily as you would hope. Gentleness that is sensitive and reassuring starts from an understanding about what is going on in someone's heart and mind.

Gentleness involves putting someone else's needs above your own. It requires putting on one side your own sense of emotional angst, aggravation or frustration. Gentleness flows from an attitude of mind that respects and upholds the other person and does not seek to deflate or undermine them.

For many people Her Majesty Queen Elizabeth epitomizes graciousness and gentleness. Those who have worked with her treasure the quality and clarity of her thinking and her ability to relate effectively to such a diverse range of people. Her gentleness enhances her impact and does not dilute it.

For a period I was the Principal Private Secretary to Sir Keith Joseph who was an influential Cabinet Minister when Margaret

Thatcher was the UK Prime Minister. He was one of the most courteous and generous-hearted people I have ever worked with. He had clear political and intellectual views which were not always popular, but those colleagues and politicians from different spheres who knew him well respected his gentleness and courteousness at a personal level. However much they disagreed with him, they were always willing to listen and engage with him because of his personal gentleness and generosity.

Individuals who bring a gentle approach can often be surprisingly influential. There is a natural tendency to mirror the approach of the people you are talking to. If someone presents their argument in a gentle and thoughtful way the natural response is to present your point of view in a similar way. This type of approach often leads to a greater willingness to modify opinions and move to an agreed way forward. In contrast if an argument is put in very robust direct terms the most likely response is one expressed in a similar way, with the result that the prospect of finding a shared, middle ground becoming much reduced.

There is truth in the pertinent verse from Proverbs that, 'A gentle answer turns away wrath'. The leader who can hold steady in the face of anger and then gently and coherently set out their case has more chance of being heard once someone has vented their anger and frustration and has calmed down.

Gentleness can involve pacing conversations and decision-making down so there is the opportunity to reflect and not be bouncing yourself and others into particular outcomes. Gentleness might involve encouraging the other person to set out a way forward and to be clear on timescales.

Jenny was increasingly fed up with the fact that her colleagues would not listen to her. She thought that her quiet, gentle approach was having no impact. At times she was reluctant to contribute but always made sure that she did offer a comment. When there was a feedback exercise in which team members commented on their colleagues she was surprised how many of their observations were about her persuasive influence.

Jenny was described as someone who always made her points in a thoughtful and carefully ordered way. There was a sensitivity about the likely impact of the points she was making and an awareness of how others were likely to respond. Her colleagues recognized that there was a gentleness in Jenny's tone and approach but did not consider that this undermined her contribution. They encouraged her to be willing to be more assertive in some of the comments she made while encouraging her to continue to make those comments in an empathetic and supportive way.

For reflection

- When have you observed gentleness being key to someone's contribution and impact?
- When have you used a gentle and thoughtful approach and it has led to people changing their views and actions?
- When have you seen gentleness 'turn away wrath' and how might you embody that type of approach?

5

Reconciliation

The most frequent reference to reconciliation is within families. A charity like Relate has had huge impact encouraging reconciliation both within couples and within families. There has been a growing emphasis on reconciliation within communities. The Truth and Reconciliation Commission set up by Nelson Mandela made a massive contribution helping to move the people of South Africa on from hate into a greater sense of shared aspiration for the future.

There is a risk of undervaluing the concept of reconciliation in a work environment. Employees and volunteers are expected to be grown-ups and get on with their lives, even if some of the interactions at work have been painful and unnecessarily aggressive.

Reconciliation at work is seen as a last resort when relationships have completely broken down. Often this is too late. If a conflict had been identified at an earlier stage and handled differently the need for a significant intervention seeking to engineer reconciliation would be much reduced.

Reconciliation, if it is working well, starts as soon as issues begin to arise between individuals or within a group. What helps is spotting unhealthy conflict early, naming it and encouraging participants and those affected to address the causes of conflict in a detached and constructive way.

The theme of reconciliation runs right through the Old and New Testaments. Isaiah talks of a future world where nation will not take up sword against nation and where people will not be trained for war any more. Isaiah writes graphically about beating swords into ploughshares and spears into pruning hooks. Proverbs talks of practical ways of bringing reconciliation, for example, 'the wise in heart are called discerning, and gracious words promote instruction'. In contrast 'the perverse stir up dissention and gossips separate close friends' with 'the violent enticing neighbours and leading them down a path that is not good'.

Jesus advises his followers to be reconciled with someone who has something against them before they offer a gift at the altar. Jesus urges them to seek to be reconciled with an adversary before going to the magistrate. Paul writes to the Corinthians about the work of reconciliation. He urges his readers not to lose heart and encourages them to see themselves as part of the ministry of reconciliation and as God's ambassadors. He encourages them both to be reconciled with God and to exercise reconciliation so there is a new creation with the old having gone, with the opportunity to build the new going forward.

Exercising a ministry of reconciliation involves listening well, discerning thoughtfully and responding with care. The advice of St Benedict was, 'listen and attend with the ear of your heart'. There is a wonderful Columbian proverb, 'keep your ear so close to the ground that you can hear the grass grow'. The solid ground for reconciliation is listening well, using the ear of the heart with a degree of openness and concentration which means we hear the grass grow.

Discerning thoughtfully is about listening for what is really going on below the surface and what the underlying issues might be. When we discern thoughtfully we are bringing peripheral vision to seek to understand what is going on. There is a Chinese proverb, 'it is not the size of the mountain that distorts our way:

it is the pebble in the shoe'. Discerning well involves spotting the irritant which may or may not be readily recognized and disposed of.

John Paul Lederach has been involved in reconciliation work across the world. For him reconciliation is not about 'forgive and forget'. For him reconciliation is about 'remember and change'. If the message is only about 'forgive and forget' the underlying issues or relations are not tackled. If the focus is on 'remember and change' there is the prospect of more fundamental reflection and the opportunity for an irreversible shift in beliefs and attitudes.

The prophet Isaiah talks about a God who blocks out transgressions and remembers your sins no more. Isaiah sees as a corollary to forgiveness the importance of reviewing the past and talking issues through together. Reconciliation that leads to sustained change will always involve honest exploration of what has happened in the past and a willingness to address seriously mistakes and learning so that there can be a genuine shift in attitude and behaviour.

A good manager will be spotting potential problems early. They may well be talking with individuals alone or together. They will be helping them explore:

- What is going on for the other person?
- What has been the cause of times of aggravation?
- What is the pebble in the shoe that might be causing the irritation?
- What type of conversation is most likely to lead to honest reflection about the best next steps?
- What two practical steps might you take to build understanding and reduce the risk of painful conflict?

Helen observed that when she talked about her work with a friend she kept returning to a difficult relationship with a colleague called Henry. Her friend thought she was in danger of building up a small problem into a major issue. Helen took every remark that Henry made as personal criticism. Her friend saw how Helen was exaggerating each small comment into a major criticism. Henry was becoming an increasingly ogre-like figure in Helen's mind.

Helen's friend recognized that this mind-set could only get worse unless it was tackled deliberately: she felt that Helen was quite enjoying complaining about Henry and did not particularly want to face up to the need to address this working relationship. Her friend became increasingly direct with Helen suggesting that unless she sought to change the working relationship with Henry, misunderstandings would be increasingly likely, with the risk that her staff may begin to take sides.

Helen decided to be very open with Henry and suggested that some informal coaching might help them to understand one another better. Helen did not want to use the language of mediation as that would sound as if their positions were more entrenched than they probably were. A coach created a suitable environment for them to talk together reflectively and through the use of some open-ended questions she prompted honest conversation. It was not long before Helen and Henry were smiling about their mis-understandings and became much more committed to working closer together. They committed to tell each other when any sense of conflict or competition arose between them. This agreement helped them identify the risks of misunderstanding at an early stage.

For reflection

- When have you been in danger of turning innocent comments from others into harsh criticism?
- How much do you see reconciliation as part of your role as a leader or manager?
- How far would you go in seeking to build a greater level of mutual understanding and reconciliation, and when would you draw in specialists such as coaches or mediators?
- How helpful is it to see aggravation as like a pebble in the shoe?
- If reconciliation is about 'remember and change' and not just about 'forgive and forget' how best do you enable people to create an irreversible shift in their attitudes and beliefs?

6

Vulnerability

Is vulnerability a weakness or a strength? Headlines often imply that vulnerability is a serious weakness: for example, 'Around 40% of a retailers' business is vulnerable to Amazon' and 'Five industries most vulnerable to digital disruption'. Personal vulnerability is considered a liability for leaders. The accepted norm is that it is difficult to lead, negotiate or make demands from a position of perceived vulnerability.

Fragility and vulnerability are at the heart of Christian understanding. Jesus entered the world not as a king or military ruler but as a helpless baby. The Gospels describe God sending his Son into the world as an innocent, helpless, fragile and vulnerable infant. Jesus walked into situations where he would be vulnerable rather than away from danger. He entered Jerusalem knowing that there were those in authority who wanted to see him dead.

Jesus engaged with the vulnerable. The first people who met Jesus as a new born child were the shepherds who lived a fragile and vulnerable existence. In his adult ministry Jesus engaged with those who were vulnerable through medical conditions, poverty, their work or lifestyle.

The Christian Gospel encourages us to recognize the fruits that grow in vulnerability. Henri Nouwen in *Bread for the Journey* writes: 'there is a great difference between successfulness and fruitfulness. Success comes from strength, control and respectability. A successful person has the energy to create something, to keep control over its development and to make it available in large quantities. Success brings many rewards and often fame. Fruits, however, come from weakness and vulnerability, and fruits are unique. A child is the fruit conceived out of vulnerability, community is the fruit borne through shared brokenness, and intimacy is the fruit that grows from touching each other's wounds. Let's remind one another that what brings us true joy is not successfulness but fruitfulness'.

Henri Nouwen talks of the preciousness of life: 'not because it is unchangeable like a diamond but because it is vulnerable like a little bird. To love life means to love its vulnerability, asking for care, attention, guidance and support. Life and death are connected by vulnerability. The new born child and the dying elder both remind us of the preciousness of our lives. Let's not forget the preciousness and vulnerability of life during the times we are powerful, successful and popular'.

Through our fragility and vulnerability we understand more about the preciousness of life. Through our vulnerability we often learn about mercy, forgiveness and reconciliation. Living with our vulnerability means recognizing we are not the finished article. We are on a continuous journey of learning and understanding. It involves being self-aware of our fragility and vulnerability and not deluding ourselves about our goodness or perfection.

Growing through fragility and vulnerability includes taking responsibility for our actions. It requires us to choose our attitudes and actions and not allow ourselves to become victims of circumstance or to blame others for our own misfortunes.

We learn so much from what has gone wrong, perhaps we can even be thankful for fragility and vulnerability because of what we learn through adversity. There is a growing understanding that the popular perception of vulnerability as a bad thing is a myth. In her article in the September 2014 edition of the *Harvard Business Review*, Emma Seppala suggests that vulnerable leaders inspire, are more authentic and build bonds that lead to increased performance.

Brené Brown in *Daring Greatly: how the courage to be vulnerable transforms the way we live, love, parent and lead*, argues that vulnerability is engaging in life, being all in, dedicating yourself to something. Embracing vulnerability means having the courage to face your fears and the wild uncertainty of the future. The vulnerable leader is deciding to meet uncertainty with an open heart, willing to experience all the ups and downs that come with it.

Augusto Giacoman, a Director with PwC based in New York, talks of how vulnerable leaders know how they can confront brutal reality head on. He suggests that vulnerability inspires teams, is required for authenticity, and allows for building greater bonds and increasing emotional connections. He emphasizes the link between vulnerability and authenticity, suggesting that authenticity means being open and honest about your beliefs and values. This includes admitting mistakes, showing emotion and not hiding behind a manufactured facade. Augusto's fundamental point is that it is impossible to be authentic without being willing to be vulnerable.

Augusto suggests that when leaders are vulnerable they are more open and emotionally available, which creates more bonding opportunities and improves team performance. He recognizes that in seeking to connect with our inner vulnerability we face a significant obstacle. We are socialized, educated and trained to build up our defences against vulnerability. This means we have to consciously build a capacity to be vulnerable which is a counter-intuitive and uncomfortable undertaking. Augusto contrasts vulnerable leaders who inspire with authenticity and humanity, with tough leaders who may inspire through fear or intimidation.

Emma Seppala (*Harvard Business Review*, September 2014) suggests that we feel more comfortable around someone who is authentic and vulnerable because we are particularly sensitive to signs of trustworthiness in leaders. She suggests that people respond to a leader who acknowledges their vulnerability because a sense of empathy creates enhanced activation in parts of the brain related to positive emotion and social connection.

Often my work as a coach involves helping individuals and teams explore areas of vulnerability. My approach is always to encourage people to be honest with themselves about these areas, open in addressing them with colleagues, and open to what they are learning about themselves and their reactions in particular situations.

Through exploring areas of vulnerability insights can grow about handling those vulnerabilities and sensitivities, alongside a greater capacity to work effectively with others with similar vulnerabilities. As we learn to understand and handle our vulnerabilities we become increasingly authentic and honest as leaders and more likely to have committed and energized followers.

On the other hand if we let our vulnerabilities get the better of us and show no sign of living with them or addressing them effectively, then the emotional connectivity with others can drain quickly. Being open about vulnerabilities needs to be accompanied by clarity about how we are approaching them if we are to be seen as both authentic and responsible.

James knew that he was vulnerable to criticism. He would turn a minor critical comment into a much bigger deal. His confidence could easily be damaged when he built up a criticism into something much bigger than was justified. James wanted feedback and was willing to learn through his mistakes, but he knew that feedback needed to be given and received in a particular way to be constructive for him.

James was open with his team about wanting feedback and needing to receive it in a way that felt constructive. James was open about his vulnerability to receiving criticism which, if delivered in a particular way, could put him into a spiral of dejection. James' team respected him for being open about this vulnerability. They developed a pattern whereby there was a genuine openness about the learning from things that had not gone well.

Because James had been open about this vulnerability to how feedback was given this led to the team having a clear and constructive procedure for giving feedback to each other in a way that would be constructively received.

For reflection

- Who have you observed expressing vulnerability in a way that has built your respect and commitment?
- How readily are you able to see your own vulnerability as a source of insight and strength rather than just a weakness?
- What vulnerabilities are you willing to share with your colleagues and how might that help build constructive working relationships going forward?
- What have you learnt from times when you have not handled your vulnerabilities as well as you had hoped?

7

Hope

Every human being needs to have a sense of hope for the future. Hope is a psychological necessity if someone is going to be able to think and move positively into their own future.

Hope, though, can be a painful slave driver if success is seen as a very precise outcome. For example, those captive in prisoner of war camps who believed fervently that they would be freed by Christmas would often suffer acute depression when their release never came by their anticipated date. A sense of hope is important for all in leadership roles as they encourage others to look forward with anticipation and expectation. For hope to be realistic it needs to be about possibilities rather than certainties, but to be convincing it has to be rooted in a genuine commitment that there will be a future, positive state.

The ancient world saw hope as a temporary illusion rather than a virtue. The clear biblical theme is of a hope grounded in a belief in a living God. Hope is viewed not as a matter of temperament nor purely conditioned by prevailing circumstances. Paul describes Abraham as, 'in hope' believing 'against hope' that he would become the father of many nations.

In the Proverbs the writer keeps emphasizing the link between wisdom and hope. The reader is encouraged to let their heart be wise and not envy others. The writer makes clear that there is a future hope for you and that your hope will not be cut off. Jeremiah when writing about the restoration of Israel talks about the Lord having plans to 'prosper you and not harm you and to give you hope and a future'.

There is no explicit reference to hope in the teaching of Jesus. He does teach his disciples not to be anxious about the future because that future is in the hands of a loving Father. He leads them to expect that after his resurrection renewed spiritual power will be available for them, enabling them to do even greater works than he did. The resurrection of Jesus revitalized their hope for the future.

In the Epistles there is a frequent association of hope with love and faith. In his Epistle to the Romans Paul addresses the suffering that his heroes were experiencing. He described suffering as producing perseverance, perseverance leading to character and character leading to hope.

Paul encourages his readers to be joyful in hope, patient in affliction and faithful in prayer. His overriding message to his readers in Romans is that the God of hope would fill them with joy and peace so they may overflow with hope.

Peter in his first Epistle talks of a living hope which flows from the resurrection of Jesus Christ and an inheritance that can never perish, spoil or fade. He encourages his readers to keep their minds alert with a firm hope about the future. Peter's hope is rooted in a God who has revealed who he is through the life and work of Jesus.

Leaders are often called upon to 'hope against hope'. In tough times the leader needs to paint a picture about what is possible going forward identifying what are believable points of reference. When a mountain is to be climbed the summit is often not visible. There is a reasonable hope that the summit exists and is attainable.

The mountain guide is expressing with certainly where the route is and the feasibility of reaching the destination. It is a confident hope in what is possible that enables the walker or climber to move through their own exhaustion and reach the desire outcome.

The leader who describes a journey as easy without obstacle might have many followers, but the leader who is sustaining followers will be combining a clear sense of hope about the future alongside realism. They will not pretend that the journey will be straightforward, but they will be describing a sense of possibility and seeking to capture the imagination about vistas and opportunities ahead.

The New Testament writers link together hope with faith and love. For any leadership venture to work well there needs to be faith in the value of the enterprise, an emotional rapport between colleagues, alongside a strong sense of delivering an outcome that turns hope into reality.

Emma was leading a project to reorganize the work of a charity, and was receiving a lot of scepticism from employees of the charity. They had organized the work of the charity in a similar way for a number of years. Many people saw no need to change even though the revenues of the charity were beginning to dip. The reaction of many people was focused on keeping going and not allowing worries about the future to alter their previous way of doing things.

Emma was careful to build a clear picture about the future opportunities that would flow from a different way of organizing the activities of the charity. She sought to build a sense of belief in what was possible. Emma was meticulous in the way she built relationships with her colleagues and showed her concern for them recognizing that new arrangements could be disruptive for them in lots of ways. Emma was rigorous in describing a positive and hopeful future for the charity continuing to meet the needs of people it was set up to serve. Emma was seeking to link together the themes of faith, love and hope in the way she sought to bring sceptical people along with her.

For reflection

- What has helped you 'bring hope against hope' and kept you going in tough times?
- When have you been able to describe a future hope of possibility and opportunity that has been convincing and motivating?
- What might be the links between faith, love and hope in the way you lead and influence others?
- How best do you balance a positive sense of hope about the future with realism in your own narrative as a leader?

8

Joy

There is a big difference between jollity and joy. Jollity is a sense of fun and excitement associated with parties or group outings. Jollity is transitory and can feel superficial.

Joy is a much deeper sense of fulfilment and connectivity with those around you. It is normally associated with work or engagement that feels particularly worthwhile. It takes longer to build up than jollity but is more sustainable. Joy brings its own source of energy and rubs off on others in a more substantive way than jollity.

The good manager is seeking to develop within their team a sense of satisfaction about the work being done. They are seeking to provide clarity of purpose enabling people to feel a sense of satisfaction and fulfilment in their work. This sense of doing something worthwhile can lead to a secure sense of joy in their work provided the expectations are reasonable and the degree of support from others is consistent and encouraging.

When you enter the domain of a team you can often sense whether the overall atmosphere is purposeful and joyful, or downbeat and flat. Seeking to create a sense of purposefulness and joy pays dividends for any manager both in terms of their own satisfaction and in terms of the effective engagement within and productivity of a team.

In both the Old Testament and the New Testament joy is considered a characteristic of an individual and of a corporate body. It is a quality grounded upon God and derived from him. The Psalms are full of references to joy with comments like, 'let me ever sing for joy', 'my heart leaps for joy', 'the joy of the whole earth' and 'the joy of your salvation'. Joy is associated with both festivals and enthronements and more personal expressions when sorrow is turned into joy. In Proverbs joy is associated with promoting peace, a cheerful approach, apt replies and the bringing of wisdom and insight.

Joy is a frequent refrain in the New Testament. The angel is recorded as saying to the shepherds, 'I bring you good news of great joy that will be for all the people'. Peter encourages his disciples to be willing to leap for joy. When the seventy-two were sent out to every town where Jesus was to go they returned with joy.

When Jesus was talking about his death and resurrection he talked about the disciples' grief turning into joy. He describes a woman giving birth and living through pain who then forgets the anguish because of her joy that the child is born.

Joy is a continuous refrain in the Epistles. James links joy and perseverance. Peter talks about inexpressible and glorious joy. John writes about proclaiming what he has seen and heard so that the joy of his hearers might be complete. He describes how there is no greater joy than hearing that his children are walking the truth.

Creating a sense of purpose and joy in any team requires deliberate thought and action. A sense of joy does not happen by chance. Jollity might flow from opening a few bottles of wine. A sense of purpose and joy flows from a quality of clear thought and engagement that leads to an emotional security that is sustainable.

A state of joy can include fun, conversation, reflection, and sadness. For example, there will be a sadness when a good colleague leaves a team, alongside the joy that flows from a constructive working relationship.

The joy of parenthood flows from long-term, consistent investment resulting in a child growing in understanding and independence. Similarly joy in a working environment is a consequence of long-term investment in building a shared endeavour alongside a consensus about desired behaviours and shared values.

When events derail a team the leader has a responsibility to protect and reshape the sense of joy in the team. Joy is not just about celebrating events of the past: it also seeks to look forward through and beyond potentially destabilizing events. Joy flows from the quality of relationships and an agreed way of tackling issues, rather than being on an instant high following good news or a depressing low in the light of bad news.

Joy is infectious. One person I work with is consistently enthusiastic, exuding a sense of purpose and joy. Initially it can feel like relentless enthusiasm but when people get to know the person concerned they recognize that there is an inner sense of joy that permeates all she does. It is infectious and people love working with her.

When someone is able to fully embrace a deep sense of inner joy they become a lynchpin in the way a team behaves. People feed on that joy recognizing that it will help them handle good times and bad and equip them to better withstand unpredictable and potentially destructive events.

In my coaching work I will often ask people to score out of ten their current levels of both fulfilment and joy in their work. I will then ask them what needs to happen for that score to rise by a couple of points. This gives useful indicators about priorities in their use of time and energy.

When George took over the project team he took care to seek to understand what motivated each member of his team. He asked them what gave them fulfilment in their work and what gave them joy in their different activities. He sought to build on this understanding of the links for each person between fulfilment and joy.

George also sought to build a picture about what caused their joy at work to be dented. After a few weeks he asked people in the team meeting to describe to their colleagues what had recently increased both their level of frustration and joy in their work. He did this in order that each member of the team understood more about their colleagues.

George invited his team to think through how they would respond to events that could potentially derail them and how they might preserve that sense of fulfilment and joy through difficult and unpredictable periods. Thinking ahead in this way equipped the team to be better prepared for future events.

For reflection

- What is the distinction you draw between jollity and joy?
- When have you experienced deep-seated joy in your work and what enabled that to happen?
- How best do you build a sense of fulfilment and joy among the people you work with?
- How best do you hold on to a sense of joy for both yourself and your team in the face of unpredictable and potentially disruptive events?

PART TWO
Head

This section focuses on themes that flow out of careful and rigorous thinking. They require us to be honest with ourselves, fair-minded and tough. The section starts with truth and considers the relevance of crucifixion, healing and humility. It then looks at freedom and judgement, and then peace and self-control.

Every leader will recognize these themes as key to leading well. The big challenge is balancing these themes so that judgement is exercised with humility, and truth is applied in a way that seeks to bring healing. Applying both freedom and self-control is at the heart of exercising responsible leadership and building followership.

9

Truth

As a junior UK civil servant in the 1970s I was often preparing answers to parliamentary questions. It was drummed into me that every answer had to be truthful. You might have concluded in drafting an answer that the Minister would not want to give a lot of detail, but without exception Ministers recognized that answers had to be truthful. There might sometimes have been a desire to be economical with the truth, i.e. not give as much detail as the questioner would have liked, but there was a shared understanding between civil servant and Minister that untruths or lies should never be placed on the parliamentary record.

This focus on truthfulness was part of the training as a junior civil servant. As I moved into more senior roles I became conscious that sometimes you played a role as a conscience. It was important to focus discussion with and submissions to Ministers on what the evidence said. Being true to the evidence was central to building credibility with colleagues and external partners. It was also critical to building relationships of trust with Ministers who expected you to understand the relevant evidence and be able to communicate it in an intelligent and comprehensible way.

One Secretary of State whom I have got to know recently commented to me that what he most appreciated about one of his Director Generals was his willingness to give him clear, unequivocal evidence and an honest perspective. This Secretary of State recognized that it was not easy for an official to say to a Minister that their approach was not soundly based. What this Secretary of State appreciated about this trusted advisor was his willingness to tell truth to power. This individual was tactful in how he made points to the Secretary of State which the politician did not want to hear. It was the combination of truthfulness and tact that enabled this Director General to be influential with the Secretary of State who always listened carefully to his views.

There are many examples of organizations where individuals have told their bosses what the bosses wanted to hear irrespective of the evidence. Every senior person wants the approval of their staff and their endorsement of the boss's favoured view. There are innumerable examples where the reinforcement of misconceived or out of date views has ultimately led to disaster. Telling the truth, however painful, is essential if an organization is going to face up to issues that have to be addressed honestly and robustly. Thankfully most organizations have checks and balances in place which ensure that facts and trends have to be faced up to. This might flow from the role of non-executive directors, auditors, external inspectors or the media.

There is a risk in many organizations of one interpretation of the truth being legitimized by a strong leader. The best leaders are combining a strength of vision and intent, alongside a belief in the importance of honesty, openness and continual re-evaluation of the evidence. The best of leaders are recognizing that there is no monopoly of truth held by one person. They are open to how facts and situations can be seen differently by different people, with truth having many different dimensions and interpretations.

Truthfulness is seen as a strong virtue in Jewish and Christian thinking. Various Psalms refer to speaking the truth from the heart: the hearers are invited to walk in the truth, desire truth and speak the truth. Proverbs suggests that truthful lips endure for ever but a lying tongue lasts only a moment. In Proverbs a truthful witness is described as saving lives with a false witness being deceitful. The focus on truthfulness is evident through the prophets. God exhorts Jeremiah to go to Jerusalem and search through the city: if he can find one person who deals honestly and seeks the truth God says he will forgive that city.

In the first chapter of John's Gospel where John is talking about the Word becoming flesh he describes Jesus as coming from the Father full of grace and truth. John is linking together grace and truth as two key characteristics of Jesus' teaching and mission.

Combining grace and truth is part of being a mindful leader embodying Christian wisdom. Grace is about understanding, empathy and forgiveness. Truth is about honesty, clarity and evidence. The best of leaders are combining grace and truth, recognizing that this can be a painful process when difficult messages have to be given. They may be accused of lacking grace when they tell the truth. When grace and forgiveness are dominant they may be accused of not facing up to the truth, hence the importance of holding grace and truth in balance together.

Janet was a trusted member of the Finance Department who would regularly monitor projected income and expenditure. She observed that the order book was thinner than it had been in recent months. The current cash flow was fine but Janet could foresee difficulties ahead. Janet did not want to dent the motivation of the senior leaders in the business but she was concerned that they were not facing up to the consequences of some of the financial realities. She began with some gentle questions to her boss about his views on the financial situation. She felt brushed aside and did not know whether this meant her boss did not see the potential difficulties or did not want to face up to the impending difficulties.

Janet wrote a summary note about the finances once a month and decided that she should put clearly in her next note the risks that she was identifying. Janet was concerned that she might be viewed as being critical or disloyal, hence she included positive things that were happening as well as questioning the financial results projected forward. Janet prepared the way with a couple of people about the issues that her paper was going to raise.

In a group meeting about her paper she was unequivocal in her concerns. In the first discussion there was a scepticism about her views with further data being requested. By the second discussion her colleagues recognized that corrective action was needed. Janet was commended for her focus on the truth alongside the graceful and firm way in which she had got her colleagues to think into some of the issues more clearly.

For reflection

- How best do you handle bringing evidence and truth to your colleagues that they might not welcome?
- How do you combine grace and truth so that you are demonstrating both understanding about how hard messages are likely to be received alongside clearly addressing difficult evidence?
- How do you speak 'truth to power' in a way that enhances trust and does not destroy working relationships?
- How do you help people to see the truth about what is happening without feeling the need to bludgeon them into submission?

10

Crucifixion

We live in an era when newspapers and social media campaigns seek to crucify people. These crucified individuals might have made a mistake, or been the leader of an organization where someone has made a mistake, or they might represent views that are very different to the views of the critics.

When in 2016 a UK newspaper branded three High Court judges as 'enemies of the people' it appeared to be seeking to crucify people with judicial responsibility who they did not agree with. Thankfully this attempt to crucify the reputation of three senior judges was rapidly seen to be spurious and ill-conceived.

The urging of the noisy crowds in Jerusalem to 'crucify him' were impassioned expressions of crowd behaviour fuelled by aggressive, threatening and hateful leaders who wanted to remove somebody whose teaching was threatening their power base.

There is relevant learning through watching out for language that builds up a sense of hysteria whereby the resulting rhetoric, and often intent, is to crucify someone's reputation and contribution. When we see crowds, either physically or through social media, building up a sense of indignation that is teetering on the edge of seeking to crucify someone's reputation, we need to observe, stand back and express our own independent view, without being overwhelmed by group think and potential hostility.

Within the New Testament the symbol of the cross is seen

as overcoming sin and death. In Paul's letter to the Colossians he talks of the cross disarming the power of authorities because Jesus overcame sin and death through the cross and then the resurrection. Jesus recognized that he needed to go to Jerusalem and face into the hostility of the Jewish authorities. He did not shirk this task: he faced into the likelihood of humiliation and death. He was not deflected from his intent.

Sometimes leadership involves facing into reality and going into hostile places where people may want to crucify us. It may be into the staff room, the board room, the staff meeting, or a parliamentary select committee. We may need to be prepared to be misunderstood, vilified and humiliated. What matters is that we understand why we are doing what we are doing and are basing our words and actions on clear evidence and a thought-through perspective. Even though others may want to crucify us we are living out our integrity and are seeking to be consistent in applying our values.

There are various references in the Gospels to Jesus encouraging his disciples to take up their cross and follow him. As part of his teaching of the twelve disciples Jesus is clear that whoever wants to be a disciple must deny themselves and take up their cross daily and follow him.

Taking up your cross in your leadership context might be about recognizing the weight of expectation that others have of you in the role. It might mean accepting the burden of responsibility you carry on behalf of a range of different people. It certainly involves recognizing that there is a weight or burden you carry on behalf of others where you do not want to let them down. Carrying a cross involves being deliberate about how you carry this weight and being resilient in the way you keep moving forward and do not give up.

There are moments when we want to crucify ourselves. We might feel we have let others down and are intensely remorseful. There are times when we want to leave behind elements of our approach or behaviour. We want to amputate a self-belief or approach that gets in the way and inhibits us. We want that part of us to die and be renewed. A desire to bruise ourselves, to self-flagellate, can lead to physical or emotional self-harm which is destructive of ourselves and others. On the other hand being clear what aspect of our approach or attitude we want to amputate and crucify can release the rest of our heart and mind to be renewed and refreshed going forward.

The cross represents a very powerful symbol of resolve amidst hate. Martin Luther King in a book entitled, *A Gift of Love* says that every time he looks at the cross he is reminded of the beauty of sacrificial love and the majesty of unswerving devotion to truth. He says, 'I can never turn my eyes from that cross without also realizing that it symbolizes a strange mixture of greatness and smallness, of good and evil. As I behold that uplifted cross I am reminded not only of the unlimited power of God but also of the sordid weakness of man. I think not only of the radiance of the divine, but also of the tang of the human. I am reminded not only of Christ at his best but also of man at his worst. We must see the cross as the magnificent symbol of love conquering hate and of light overcoming darkness, but in the midst of this glowing affirmation, let us never forget that our Lord and Master was nailed to that cross because of human blindness. Those who crucified him knew not what they did'.

Martin Luther King does not vilify those who sought to crucify Jesus. He described them as not knowing what they did. His message was about seeking to bring light to overcome darkness with love having the potential of conquering hate.

Bob felt that he was being crucified by some of his colleagues. He felt their disapproval intensely. He wanted to hit back and undermine their reputation, yet he knew that this would only make matters worse. He wanted to influence his critics so they stopped trying to vilify him and make him look foolish.

It felt to Bob that he was carrying a huge burden of pressure of expectation from his colleagues. It felt as if he could do nothing right and was constantly being battered by their views. It was the negative gossip that got to him: he was happy to debate the evidence in meetings but it was the insidiousness of the dismissive, private remarks that undermined his confidence.

Bob recognized that he had to keep carrying this cross. He worked hard at trying to build a positive relationship with his colleagues. He deliberately did not show resentment. He kept trying to be engaged with and supportive of others. He began to see who his allies could be when decisions were needed about how best to use the available resources within the organization. Bob held firmly on to the belief that even though it felt as if people were trying to crucify him, he needed to maintain his equilibrium and integrity and not allow his heart to be pierced, however harshly the criticisms of others seemed to pierce his self-belief.

For reflection

- How would you respond if you felt someone was seeking to crucify your reputation?
- If someone is radically opposed to your views and wants to undermine them, how might you engage with them in a constructive and firm way?
- What aspects of your attitude and approach might need to be amputated?
- What parts of your understanding of yourself and life need to die so there can be new life?

11

Healing

The focus of the work of the doctor or nurse is on healing the body. The focus of the counsellor or psychiatrist is on healing of the mind. For those involved in mediation or reconciliation there is a focus on healing of wounds. The teacher, youth worker or church minister or chaplain will see healing as part of their work where pain has distorted attitudes and created barriers to harmony.

In any sphere there will be an element of healing as part of the work of any manager. Where there are broken relationships, discord or disagreement there is a need for healing before people can move on and address new issues constructively. In order for healing to be effective it has to be deliberate with time allowed for the healing to take its course, with environmental factors ideally conducive to healing rather than continuing discord and disruption.

Because human relationships are dynamic and fragile, people can be left bruised with relationships needing healing. Often the healing is best done quietly where a leader is bringing people together and helping them work through their pain and face into the next steps. Creating healing in relationships requires sensitivity about the right type of involvement so that healing can take a natural course and not be rushed.

Physical healing requires careful treatment, the right length of time for recovery, alongside care to ensure that the wounded area is not knocked. Emotional healing similarly requires deliberate attention, the allowance of reasonable time, and a deliberate and measured approach.

The healing leader in any organization is aware of where there is hurt and pain. They are sensitive to the type of treatment that has the prospect of working which may involve giving people space to understand the perspective of others, or creating a context in which difficult issues can be talked through thoughtfully. Sometimes a leader needs to be overt, giving clear signals about expectations, whereas the healing aspect of the leadership role is often best done quietly with the individuals concerned making no fuss about what is happening.

One example I observed was a team member who had very good bilateral relationships with each of his colleagues in the executive team. Individuals talked to him when they had an issue with one of their colleagues. The consequence was that this team member became a sounding board so that other team members could work through their issues in a safe place. His was a quiet, discreet role but the consequence of his helping others to work through relationships with their colleagues meant that he had a profound effect on the wellbeing of the whole team. He was a healing leader without setting out with that intent.

Another individual was very conscious when there was disagreement between peers. She was good at inviting people into the same room together and putting them on the spot to think through the causes of their disagreement and how they could move on. When they were in the same room she was willing to challenge them explicitly about what were the causes of their disagreement, what effect did they think the disagreement was having on others, and how best might they move into a frame of mind where they were willing to tackle the issues and move on constructively.

Sometimes the healing of relationships can take a long time with persistence and patience being key. A bone that has been broken and then been re-joined may even be stronger than the original bone. Where a working relationship has been broken the healing process can enable that relationship to become even stronger than before the breakage. As individuals mend a working relationship they can become more sensitized to what might derail it going forward and how best it is developed and strengthened for the future.

Jesus brought physical, emotional and spiritual healing. He sought out the sick and the lame bringing healing and new life. Sometimes his healing work was dramatic. For example the raising of Jairus' daughter from the dead. At other times the healing was done quietly; the lady who just touched the hem of his garment felt his healing power flow into her. Jesus brought emotional healing as well as physical healing. He helped Mary and Martha understand as sisters their different perspectives and approaches. He brought healing and reassurance to the Samaritan woman at the well who felt an outcast and had suffered from a series of broken relationships.

Jesus' healing restored people to their communities; the leper was no longer an outcast. He brought spiritual healing by bringing renewal to people's minds where hopelessness was replaced with a hope for the future. One of the legacies from Jesus to the disciples was the focus on physical, emotional and spiritual healing. In the Epistles healing is described as one of the fruits of the Spirit. The gift of healing is seen as a treasured gift to be used wisely. This gift of healing embraces physical, emotional and spiritual wellbeing, allowing each individual to own their own healing process.

In the book of Proverbs healing and trustworthiness are linked together. A wicked messenger is described as falling into trouble, while a trustworthy envoy brings healing. Elsewhere in Proverbs the words of the reckless are described as piercing like a sword, while the words of the wise brings healing. The inference is that the words we say are key to bringing insight and healing. Just as the doctor may be direct in their guidance so that physical healing is allowed to happen, so the leader may need to be direct in their advocacy and steers to force a recognition that healing needs to happen.

Rashid felt like a pawn in a game of chess. There seemed to be on going disputes between her Directorate and the Finance Directorate. Information was not always shared. Timetables were often ignored. Gossip was rife. The sense of mutual support and a common goal was limited, yet the two organizations were part of the same enterprise. They needed to work together for the enterprise to be successful, but a lot of history, baggage and resentment was getting in the way.

Rashid could see the wounds from previous disputes and how they were not being allowed to heal. Rashid knew people in both Directorates and saw the good in people. She took it on herself to seek to build understanding. She invited people from different Directorates out for lunch together. She praised the good efforts and positive results. She drew attention to the best examples of joint working.

Rashid was consistent in affirming people in a way that came naturally to her and did not look forced. When she spotted a potential disagreement she encouraged the people to talk through the issue in as dispassionate a way as possible. Rashid was seeking to live out the proverb that the tongue of the wise brings healing. She was persistent and deliberate while being self-effacing. As the relationships between members of the two Directorates gradually got better, someone described Rashid as the glue that kept the two organizations working together more effectively.

For reflection

- Who do you observe being a healing leader behind the scenes and what did they do well?
- What is the emotional healing that is most needed in an organization of which you are part and what might be the next steps?
- How best do you help bring emotional healing to the part of the organization where you are a member?
- How open are you to drawing on the help of others when the healing process involves more expertise than you possess?

12

Humility

What can be damaging in any organization is false humility or excessive humility. False humility is the pretence of humility when an individual is trying to control and manipulate behind the scenes, while seeking to project an image of support and compliance. Excessive humility is where an individual identifies a problem that needs solving, or has insights that they want to offer, but does not express their view and fails to have the influence they ought to have.

We tend to see false humility as more dangerous and destructive than excessive humility. Both can be equally damaging. False humility can flow from someone's excessive belief in their own importance. Excessive humility flows from an individual under-estimating their potential influence and not recognizing the responsibility they have to speak up and share their insights.

Humility is a virtue that involves listening carefully to what others are saying, weighing up the strength of different arguments, recognizing that there are a variety of ways of tackling a particular problem, and being willing to test out thoughtfully different approaches. Humility involves bringing an accurate assessment of your strengths and less strong areas. It means being honest and acknowledging who is more effective than you in particular contexts.

Humility is about enabling others to be up front and acknowledging when they are in a better position than you to take a lead, so ensuring that the momentum is kept up on something that you believe is important. Good teamwork means putting the success of the team above the visible success of you as an individual. Humility means allowing other people to take full credit particularly if they are new to an organization or role and building up their reputation and credibility.

Humility does not mean always agreeing with those in positions of authority. You may think that what these people want is your assent all the time. What they probably most need from you is a differentiation between affirmation when they make the right choices and feedback when things do not go well. Any boss wants honest, frank views from the people working with them. Macawber-type humility, which means always saying that the boss is right, can lead to disaster if the views of a boss are not challenged in the light of new evidence.

Humility involves being comfortable in who you are. Mother Teresa once said, 'If you are humble, nothing will touch you, neither praise nor disgrace because you know what you are.' T. S. Eliott wrote, 'The only wisdom we can hope to acquire is the wisdom of humility'. The 19th-century American preacher, Phillips Brooks made this observation on false humility, 'The true way to be humble is not to stoop until you are smaller than yourself, but to stand at your real height against some higher nature that will show you what the real smallness of your greatness is'.

The Psalmist wrote, 'in your majesty ride forth victoriously in the cause of truth, humility and justice; let your right hand achieve awesome deeds'. This coupling of truth, humility and justice is core to spiritual insight. In Proverbs are thoughts that humility comes with risk, humility comes before honour, and grace is given to the humble. In Psalms the Lord is described as sustaining the humble and crowning the humble with salvation.

Jesus invites those who are weary and burdened to come to him and he will give them rest. He describes himself as gentle and humble in heart providing rest for the souls of the weary. Jesus concludes the parable of the wedding feast by saying that all those who exalt themselves will be humbled, and those who humble themselves will be exalted. Jesus talks of the importance of humility alongside the taking up of responsibility. He was equipping the disciples to have the humility to understand the context and the people around them, combined with the resolve and determination to be advocates for a new way of living. Humility was not an end in itself, it was part of equipping the disciples to be effective leaders.

Perhaps the strongest theme from the biblical texts is the interrelationship of truth, humility and justice. They go together as a triumvirate setting a tone and expectations for mindful effective leadership.

Jean prided herself on being humble, which she saw as a virtue. Her boss kept saying to her that she needed to make her presence felt. The feedback to Jean was that she had lots of good ideas. She had built clear understanding about how the regulatory body where she worked could become more effective. She knew that some of the material that the regulatory body put out was counterproductive and set the wrong tone, but Jean just assumed that her bosses knew better. Her humility was getting in the way of her making an effective contribution within the organization.

Jean's boss decided that she would take this point head-on and said to Jean that she was far too humble for her own good, and that her excess humility was getting in the way of her effectiveness. Jean wanted to be more influential in the organization and felt she had a contribution to make. The observation that she was far too humble for her own good was acceptable to her, but the criticism that her humility was damaging her effectiveness in the organization was painful. She wanted the regulatory body to be effective and wanted to play her part in developing its impact.

Jean began to talk through with a couple of good friends how she could both maintain the integrity of her humility and have the type of impact that she felt she should have in the organization. She resolved that she should speak her mind more and seek to be more influential. She would share her insights while keeping an open mind about whether those insights were valid. There was very little risk for Jean that she would switch from being humble to arrogant, but she now saw scope to push herself to make a more influential and impactful contribution.

For reflection

- What might you take forward in the cause of truth, humility and justice?
- How best do you avoid the risks of false humility or excessive modesty?
- What steps do you need to take to be more comfortable in who you are?
- How best do you stand up tall and keep an accurate assessment of who you are?

13

Freedom

As a leader we want the freedom to use our own initiative within structures that we understand and acknowledge. Every leader can feel burdened by the constraints upon them that limit their freedom. They long for the freedom to take forward the ideas that are most precious to them. But no leader can act in isolation. If they are to have an impact they will need followers who are willing to follow. For a leader to be effective they need other people around them who are willing to hear what they are advocating. It is nice to have the freedom to express your view, but if nobody wants to listen to what you have to say, the freedom to express your views does not lead to much impact.

Most leaders feel hemmed in by the structures in which they operate. They frequently do not recognize the influence they can have through their words and actions. They often have the freedom to set a tone, to make choices about the order in which priorities are tackled, alongside the freedom to choose how to influence and develop the people they engage with. The freedom to change fundamental priorities might be illusory, but there is always the freedom to choose the attitude of mind you bring which will then ripple through the organization and have a much bigger impact than you might anticipate.

The Old Testament prophets recognize the pull of freedom.

Jeremiah talks about setting slaves free after they had served for six years. Isaiah talks about proclaiming freedom for the captives and releasing prisoners from darkness. In Romans is the imagery of creation being liberated from the bondage of decay and brought into freedom. John records the words of Jesus that the truth will set you free.

In the letter to the Galatians Paul talks of the call to be free, but not in a way that uses freedom to indulge the sinful nature. Paul encourages his readers that because Christ has set us free, they should stand firm and not let themselves be burdened by the yoke of slavery. Peter talks about living as free people, but not using the freedom as a cover-up for evil. James links law and freedom recognizing that the framework of law provides freedom, but that freedom needs to be used responsibly.

The thoughtful leader is balancing freedom and responsibility toward others. They are providing clarity about future direction and expectations about the type of behaviour and interaction that will enable a team to work effectively. The resolute leader will be bringing clarity about the boundaries and the rules that need to be followed. They will be underlining the importance of proper financial and behavioural standards that have to be followed.

In parallel they will be identifying the scope of the discretion individuals have. Within the framework of agreed priorities and ways of working, maximizing the freedom people have in delivering their objectives normally reinforces their motivation.

Sometimes procedures have to be very tight with best practice followed, for example, in the way a surgical operation is done or the way police collect evidence. Accounting procedures will mean highly specified recording of data. Employment legislation requires there to be consistency in the way individuals are treated.

But there should always be some scope for freedom in ways of working which allow individuals and teams to demonstrate their initiative and take forward experimental approaches. Where there is an assumption that an approach needs to be identical to what has been done before it must be right periodically to test this presumption. The creative organization is always testing the boundaries and developing new approaches to addressing long-term issues.

Freedom should never be used as a cover-up for an individual sticking rigidly to their idiosyncratic preferences. Whenever an individual wants to try a very different way of approaching an issue it is helpful if some independent people are involved so that there is an authentication about whether a novel approach is worth taking forward.

We are often in bondage to the ways in which we have previously done things. It is a good challenge for any organization to think about how they allow people the freedom to experiment within an agreed framework. Part of the contracting will be about the sharing of results and having a careful eye to what might be the consequences on other parts of an organization of experimentation in a particular area.

Martin felt constrained by the way things had always been done in the organization. He recognized that rules related to finance and safety were crucial to follow. He appreciated that no decision should be made of wider significance to the business without consultation with those potentially affected. At times he was so conscious of the expectations upon him to abide by the norms in the organization that he did not fully appreciate the scope he had to exercise choices in his leadership role. He could give clearer signals about the type of development that his people needed to experience. There was considerable discretion about how the skills of different people were deployed to maximize the effectiveness of the team overall.

Martin increasingly came to recognize that his biggest freedom was about how he used his own time. He had the discretion to reach a view on where he could add most value. He was gradually being liberated from the bondage of feeling he had to be perfect and had to be able to do every task himself. He recognized that a key contribution that he needed to make was to be utterly rigorous about the evidence of progress so that he could bring an honest assessment of what future steps were needed. He treasured the fact that he had discretion about the use of his time. He recognized that he would have to account for the results within his area which would require him to use his time in a deliberate and measured way.

For reflection

- How much is there a risk that we do not recognize the extent of the freedom we have to make choices about priorities and the use of time?
- What practices or attitudes are we enslaved to that we need to be freed from?
- Are there times when we use our freedom as a means of avoiding taking responsibility for certain things?

14

Judgement

We are often ambivalent about the word 'judgement'. We want others to exercise good judgement on our behalf. We want to be judged fairly. We take pride in bringing clarity of thought in the way we judge the actions of others. We do not want prejudice or irrelevant factors to cloud our judgement. On the other hand we do not always want to be judged. We are reluctant to hear the message that we have failed to live up to the expectations of others. A factual assessment that puts us below a line is received as a harsh judgement that can knock our confidence and resolve. We can often avoid situations where we are going to be judged.

We are having to make judgements all the time. Is it safe to cross the road? Do I believe what the sales representative is telling me? Do I think that one person's opinion has more weight than another person's view? We are making judgements about whether we should respect a particular viewpoint and allow it to influence our perspective. We are continually making assessments about whether an individual has understood a particular task and what are the consequences if an action is not completed.

When a manager writes a performance appraisal or a reference on an individual they are likely to have in their mind a perspective about whether that individual brings sound judgement to the decisions they make. We want to develop employees, colleagues or volunteers so that they exercise judgement thoughtfully with a careful appreciation of the consequences of those judgements.

A judge in a court is weighing up the evidence and reaching a judgement in the context of the legal system in which they operate. A judgement might have very severe consequences for an individual, such as life imprisonment. The judge exercises their responsibilities in full knowledge of the evidence and with the proper scrutiny afforded by the higher courts. The judgement is rigorous and dispassionate.

Within the Judeo-Christian tradition justice and love sit alongside each other. God is described as someone who brings judgement but also as someone who brings love and compassion. In the Old Testament there is a clear focus on judging righteously and not showing partiality in judgement. God is described as someone who seeks justice and restores justice: he judges the earth and replaces wickedness with justice.

In Proverbs the reader is asked to not let wisdom and understanding out of their sight and exhorted to preserve sound judgement and discretion as they are the source of life and hope.

Jesus talks about the importance of justice with people giving account for what they have said and done. He talked of coming into the world to bring judgement. His approach was about judging having listened and bringing a judgement that is just. The Epistle to the Romans contains practical advice about the exercise of judgement: the writer talks of God's judgement being based on truth, acknowledging that when we pass judgement on others we are often condemning ourselves. We are encouraged to view ourselves with sober judgement. James links together judgement and mercy.

A leader is required to make judgements every day. Sometimes they are following a set of values and rules within an organization.

On other occasions the leader is having to apply those values and rules in new contexts where discretion is needed. The exercise of judgement is a privilege of leadership. The judgements we make affect people's lives, potentially dramatically. If an organization is not doing well there may need to be a judgement about whose employment comes to an end. If a team has not been working effectively a judgement will be needed about what changes should be made in the team for it to succeed. The exercise of judgement often leads to short-term pain and aggravation, but if the judgement is not exercised at an early stage the potential problems become more acute.

Good leadership requires a willingness to make judgements, the capacity to apply values in a discerning way, and the courage to carry out hard decisions in as constructive a way as possible. Sound leadership involves combining judgement and mercy, but it does not mean that mercy always trumps justice. Where there has been unfairness it needs to be corrected. Where there has been inappropriate behaviour, the individuals concerned need to face up to the consequences of their actions. Sound judgement that removes someone from an area of responsibility may feel harsh to the person concerned and fully justified to colleagues and perhaps long overdue to other individuals affected.

Hazel always wanted more evidence before she made a judgement about an individual. She saw the good and the potential in people and wanted to reinforce positive attributes whenever she could. Hazel recognized that she had to play a full part in the performance management arrangements which required her to rate the performance of those working with her. She found the need to make relative judgements tough, but recognized it was part of her job. This process forced Hazel to be clear on the evidence about someone's performance and whether there were any mitigating factors.

Hazel recognized that she had to be equally fair to all the people working for her, irrespective of how much she liked them as individuals. Hazel wanted to be thoughtful and merciful in the way she understood why a couple of her staff were not performing as well as she had hoped. She recognized that it was in the interests of these individuals that they heard directly and clearly from her about where they needed to further develop their contribution. It was not in their interests for Hazel to be soft in her judgement about their performance. What was important to her was to be able to find a thoughtful and persuasive way in which to put development points across.

For reflection

- When might you be at risk of being hesitant about giving a clear judgement that your role requires you to make?
- How best do you balance justice and mercy in the way you treat the people around you?
- How best do you view yourself with sober judgement?
- What are your next steps in developing the way you exercise judgement responsibly as a leader?

15

Peace

The most effective teams I work with have stimulating and engaging conversations. Dialogue can be robust and challenging but they are fundamentally at peace with themselves and each other.

In military terms peace is what happens at the end of conflict. As a leader peacefulness is about holding together different interests and recognizing the delicate balance you are seeking to maintain. The Jewish word 'shalom' implies peace that results from reaching an equilibrium rather than the absence of conflict.

If team members say they are entirely at peace with each other my first concern would be whether they are interacting with each other in a meaningful way or are they purely in their own silos. The message 'we are at peace with each other' can mean a truce whereby many underlying issues still need to be resolved.

In a good quality, mature relationship in either a personal or a working environment two people can be having honest debate and interaction which can look as if they are in dispute. They may have built an equilibrium in which they have stimulating interchange knowing that their working relationship is secure because there are moments of peacefulness that hold them together.

The Old Testament includes many battles but also emphasizes the importance of seeking peace. In Proverbs is the exhortation that those who promote peace have joy. The heart of peace is described as giving life to the body. The Psalmist records

God promising peace to his people. A future awaits those who seek peace. In the New Testament Luke starts with Zechariah's song which talks of the Messiah shining on those living in darkness and guiding their feet into the path of peace.

Jesus encouraged his disciples to bring peace to those they engaged with, while recognizing that his message might create division. The Epistles includes reference to peace as one of the fruits of the Spirit and the importance of sowing in peace in order to raise a harvest. Perhaps the best known Biblical reference to peace are the words in Philippians that the peace of God transcends all understanding and can guard your hearts and minds.

When there is disagreement and discord you want peace to break out. You want to wipe away the aggravation and allow relationships to start again. You want peace to break out with a vengeance. It can be a demanding journey to move from daily skirmishes to a more harmonious and creative working together which may require external mediation. It will certainly require one or two people within an organization to own the process of building a stronger set of behaviours and forward looking engagement. There may need to be cathartic conversations in which the causes of the regular skirmishes are exposed before there can be a move to a greater level of mutual understanding and a fresh start.

Sometimes a new objective or set of circumstances provide a common cause enabling petty disputes to become a matter of history. New shared objectives can provide a renewed focus which allows peace to break out without having to dissect what happened in the past.

Part of my work as a coach is helping people think through what will give them greatest joy and fulfilment and thereby what will help them be at peace with themselves. The leader who wants to make a difference in their chosen sphere is always going to be exposed to conflict. If they avoid conflict they are not going to be as effective as they should be. What matters is how they look after their equilibrium and bring a peace of mind as they enter situations where there is disagreement and disunity.

Building peace is never straightforward where it involves getting people to face up to their part in creating a perpetuating conflict. The bringer of peace may be described as an intruder or trouble-maker. In these situations bringing clarity about what you are seeking to achieve and your motives helps to build shared understanding. You are not trying to railroad people into submission, you are trying to help them see there is the prospect of a more creative and purposeful dialogue where the focus is looking forward rather than raking over the wrongs of the past. In doing this you are applying the belief that those who promote peace receive joy, even if that joy might be a long time coming.

Amanda felt stuck in the middle of a law practice where the solicitors seemed to be constantly bickering about each other. As the senior administrator she was often listening to their barbed comments about colleagues. There were times when some of the solicitors hardly spoke to each other. The atmosphere could feel tense and at times poisonous.

Amanda wanted peace to break out but knew that this would not happen without intervention. Amanda talked to a couple of the younger solicitors to see if they felt similarly about the atmosphere. She built an alliance with these colleagues about the need for change. Two of them plucked up the courage to talk to the senior partner about the destructive effect of the current negativity and the need for a radical shift in the way the practice operated.

With some reluctance the senior partner agreed to some external facilitation of the professional group. The first away-day began with exchanges of silence, but eventually there was a sharing of the reasons for the discord. The facilitator asked them to describe the type of working relationships that they wanted to have in the future. With some apprehension they all engaged in describing an atmosphere where there could be more harmonious working together.

By the end of the first away-day a truce had broken out. By the end of the second away-day there were some positive steps in place to build constructive ways of addressing future differences and to ensure that shared aspirations and values had a bigger impact on how the organization worked going forward.

For reflection

- What might be getting in the way of peaceful co-existence in your organization?
- What might be the relevance of the phrase in your organization, 'sow in peace and raise a harvest'?
- How might you develop your inner peace and equilibrium recognizing that 'a heart of peace gives life to the body'?
- In what ways might you guide other people's feet in the path of peace?

16

Self-control

Impressive leaders look in control of whatever situation they are in. If they are chairing a meeting they have planned how to handle the agenda and they bring a measured way of steering each item. If they are in debate with someone they look as if they have control of their own evidence and know how they are going to put across their points to best effect.

The individual who is exercising self-control is using their time and energy to good effect. They are not letting their emotions get the better of them and drive them to inconsistent and unplanned interventions. The leader who is exercising good self-control will tend to be someone who understands how they are likely to react in different situations and has planned their approach carefully so that they are able to be dispassionate whatever the provocation from others.

On the other hand excessive self-control can mean that an individual never expresses what they really think. They hide their emotions so well that others feel they cannot get to know them. This may mean that the bonds within a team are not as strong as they might be.

In Proverbs a person who lacks self-control is described as being like a city whose walls are broken through. Self-control is seen as one of the fruits of the Spirit in Galatians. In his first letter Peter urges his readers to be self-controlled and alert. In his second letter Peter talks of adding to faith, goodness; and to goodness, knowledge; and to knowledge, self-control; and to self-control, perseverance; and to perseverance, Godliness; and to Godliness, mutual affection; and to mutual affection, love. Self-control is right at the centre of this description by Peter of character. Titus suggests that those who hold leadership positions should be hospitable, love what is good, be self-controlled, upright, and holy and disciplined.

In the description of the fruits of the Spirit in Galatians, self-control is linked with love, joy, peace, patience, kindness, goodness, faithfulness and gentleness. It is the concluding characteristic of the fruits of the Spirit. Perhaps this suggests self-control underpins the proper exercise of all the other fruits of the Spirit.

The parent is seeking to develop self-control in the toddler who can appear to be fighting against every sort of authority. When youngsters hit the teenage years the hope is that enough self-control will have developed in them in order to preserve them from succumbing to the biggest risks of teenage life.

For a junior manager self-control is about focusing on their own contribution and doing their own defined role to the best possible effect.

As someone is promoted and has more people working with them they have to become much more selective in their use of time and energy. Self-control becomes increasingly important in terms of deciding how they use their time and where they intervene. At times the manager may feel they could do a role more effectively than one of the staff working for them. They are having to exercise the self-control of letting individuals learn from their own experience: self-control is about setting clear expectations and then letting an individual learn from what goes well or less well.

Self-control is the exact opposite of intervening at every available opportunity.

When discretion is given to others it is right to take a view on where are the risks that we need to keep an eye on. Where do we need to keep alert to unexpected behaviours or individuals not grasping properly what the expectations upon them are? The more senior a person becomes the greater the need for self-control in order to maximize their impact when they have a limited amount of time available. They need to develop the art of asking the right question and being present at the key conversations, without dampening the energy and commitment of people working with them.

There are moments when too much self-control can be an inhibitor. Sometimes caution has to be put on one side when firm action is needed. There are times when equivocation is exactly the wrong attitude of mind. Self-control needs to be overcome when a rapidly emerging problem needs to be addressed or action taken. Unremitting self-control can be a dangerous inhibitor to creativity and the forging of new alliances. There is a time to break out from previously accepted norms and recognize that there are new opportunities to be grasped.

Joseph enjoyed doing architectural drawings. The freedom to draw innovative designs was what he had always wanted to do through years of training as an architect. He wanted to fill every day drawing up intricate designs. But to be successful in an architectural business he had to be effective in building relationships with prospective clients and then take through designs to implementation. He needed to see the holistic contribution of the architect. He recognized he needed to apply his own self-control so that his energy and time was used to best effect to the benefit of the architectural business.

If Joseph spent all his time doing designs and drawings he would never win any business, or see his plans put into effect. Joseph forced himself to do the parts of the job he found least satisfying, sometimes through gritted teeth: he brought more self-control in the way he used his time. He also needed to come across to prospective clients as someone who wanted to talk to them rather than doing so under sufferance.

Various people in the architectural practice annoyed Joseph. In his early days he would have ignored them and sulked. He had taught himself that it was important to have relationships with people right across the business. When he was in danger of feeling annoyed he recognized that he needed to press the self-control button so that he did not let his emotions result in his acting in an unhelpful and counterproductive way.

Joseph eventually got to the point of being much more open to marketing what he was doing. He became far less inhibited in demonstrating the potential scope for innovative design. He got rid of the self-limiting self-control that had stopped him sharing his most creative idea. A key area of development for Joseph before he would become a candidate for a middle management position was this ability to control the use of his time in a way that was in the best interest of both the business and himself. Gradually he got there but it was hard work.

For reflection

- How effective is your self-control when you feel under emotional pressure?
- How best do you balance being self-controlled and being alert to what is happening around you?
- When might you be too self-controlled for your own good and for that of the organization of which you are part?
- How is a degree of self-control helping you have an effective impact within your organization?

PART THREE
Hands

This section looks at some of the applications of themes dealing with the heart and the head. It starts with responsibility leading into sacrifice, community and communion. The attributes of faithfulness, perseverance, kindness and patience are then explored.

How we embody insights from Christian wisdom alongside other insights that are important to us is the challenge of leading well in demanding times. The themes in this section are pertinent for every leader. The challenge is how do we apply them in combination so that we are exercising our responsibilities well, building community and creating an acceptance of the importance of kindness and patience, alongside sacrifice and persistence?

17

Responsibility

The effective and responsible leader recognizes the responsibilities they carry and can sit lightly to those with responsibilities. They recognize their obligations but see the boundaries around those obligations. They are willing to accept full responsibility for their actions and are also comfortable delegating responsibility to others.

You will have observed people who say they were willing to take on responsibility and want the recognition for volunteering, but somehow nothing ever happened. You want to have evidence that someone can deliver on responsibilities before you are willing to give them greater responsibility. You will also have observed people weighed down by responsibility unable to keep those responsibilities in perspectives.

The risk for many of the people I work with is that they have an overdeveloped sense of responsibility. They are committed to making a difference in the sphere in which they operate and seek evidence of where their direct intervention has made a significant difference. My task is often to enable them to reframe that sense of responsibility so that it is less about the doing of the task and more about enabling others to bring the right attitude of mind to do tasks well.

In Jesus' parable of talents, the man going on the journey entrusts his wealth to three people giving one five bags of gold, another two bags and another one, each according to their ability. The two men who were given five talents and two talents used those resources well and doubled the resources given to them. The man given one talent hid it in the ground. When the man returned from the journey he praised those who had used the talents deliberately while describing the individual who had hidden his talent as a lazy servant.

Part of the message from the story is about accepting responsibility and using responsibility wisely. Jesus is clear when talking to the Pharisees that they will be held responsible for their actions. After Judas betrays Jesus he is seized with remorse and seeks to return the thirty pieces of silver to the Chief Priest. The response of the priests to Judas was that betraying innocent blood was his responsibility.

Paul in the Corinthians talked about being responsible to God for your actions. The focus in the Judeo-Christian scriptures on accepting responsibility and using responsibilities well has resulted in successive generations being strongly influenced by this duty to take responsibility and use it well: hence the influence of Christians in the development of education, health, economic and humanitarian aid and the setting up of democratic institutions. Sometimes this sense of responsibility has turned into the imposition of a preconceived set of values and structures. On other occasions it has led to effective partnership with those who come with a different set of beliefs and cultural understandings.

Jesus believed that it was an obligation on him to go to Jerusalem and be ready to be crucified. He accepted this responsibility knowing that his death would not be the end of the story. When we face into responsibility and go into situations where we feel that our reputation, if not our life, is at risk it is reassuring to recognize that there is life beyond a painful event. We may feel as if we are likely to be crucified when attending a particular hearing or committee, but there is another phase of life beyond the inquisition.

Part of mindfulness as a leader is related to how we treat responsibility. We have responsibilities to those who have appointed us and trust us. We have responsibility to those looking to us for leadership. Their reasonable expectation is that we will make decisions having weighed up different factors carefully.

We have a responsibility to those who are following us which can sometimes feel a burden and sometimes a joy. Our responsibility is not to do other people's jobs for them. Ours is to set a direction bringing clarity and insight, steering others at the right moment and providing them with a wider perspective that draws from our experience.

When Maria walked to work she delighted in the opportunity to lead a project and enable the IT to function more effectively in the insurance company. She was thrilled to hold this leadership role and enjoyed the opportunity to influence others and devise a much better system than had operated before. She knew there would be tough moments when others would blame her for lack of progress. She knew that she would have to carry responsibility for the whole project and protect some people from feeling that burden of responsibility as she knew the weight of responsibility would dampen their creativity and effectiveness. There would be occasions when she would be protecting someone from criticism and at the same time having frank conversations with them about how they were going to take forward the commitments they had made and the responsibility on their shoulders.

Maria was painfully aware that if something went wrong she would be held responsible. Maria recognized that she had to fully embrace that responsibility and sit lightly to it. If the project took longer than originally planned that would not be the end of the world. Maria recognized that she was learning and developing all the time and building wider networks. Some things would go better under her watch than others. She needed to bring a realism about what she was responsible for and how others would interpret differing situations.

Maria kept telling herself that she must not get too bogged down feeling a huge weight of responsibility upon her. She needed to keep fresh and be mindful of other aspects of her life that were important to her thereby keeping her work responsibilities in perspective. Yes, her work was important, but it was only one part of her life. She felt an obligation to use her talents well, but she had learnt from experience that if she got too sucked into these responsibilities, then she would become emotionally and physically exhausted. Being a mindful leader meant embracing and enjoying her responsibilities while not being completely dominated or overwhelmed by them.

For reflection

- How do you best embrace your responsibilities and sit lightly to them?
- How best do you experience a responsibility as a joy rather than a burden?
- What helps you sit lightly to responsibilities?
- How best do you handle a situation where you are beginning to feel overwhelmed by your responsibilities?

18

Sacrifice

The leader under pressure might be thinking about the priorities at work they need to sacrifice in order to ensure the most important priorities are delivered. They might on occasion be considering which personal preferences they need to sacrifice in time in order to deliver on the expectations from others at work. There are likely to be moments when a leader is reflecting on what they need to sacrifice in terms of personal ambition in order to fulfil their responsibilities towards their family.

There will have been occasions for most leaders when they made a mistaken decision that had unfortunate consequences. There may be an initial inclination to hide the consequences of the issue or to blur the personal responsibility for the decision that led to the unfortunate consequences. For every leader there will be occasions when something has gone wrong in their area of responsibility for which they were accountable overall. They may not have been aware of the issue or problem but they recognize that it happened under their watch.

There will be times when a leader has to be willing to take responsibility for mistakes they have made or for errors that have happened under their watch. They may need to offer themselves as a sacrifice so that the organization can move on. After a file including a significant amount of personal data was lost deep in an organization, the chief executive decided to resign because the error happened under their watch. To the individual this action was the right thing to do. To some others this was a bigger personal sacrifice than was needed. A consequence was that this individual became a wise mentor to many individuals over the subsequent decade who were living with big responsibilities and unpredictable risks.

Sacrifice is a key theme in the Judeo-Christian tradition. In the Old Testament sacrifice is part of the routine and ritual of life. It provided a reminder of the gift of life to the people as they brought regular gift offerings to sacrifice. There was an underlying theme about how sacrifice is offered and the intent behind it. In Proverbs there are references to the Lord detesting the sacrifice of the wicked, especially when it is brought with evil intent. The Old Testament writers put sacrifice into a wider context. In Hosea the Lord is described as desiring mercy, not sacrifice, and an acknowledgement of God rather than burnt offerings. In Ecclesiastes the hearers are asked to listen rather than to offer the sacrifice of fools who do not know what they are doing.

When Jesus was calling his disciples he said he desired mercy and not sacrifice. Sacrifice was not an end in itself. It was part of a holistic way of embracing faith and life. The Epistle writers talk of Jesus having sacrificed himself for others. In a unique way Jesus' death was a sacrifice of atonement which created the scope for new life and hope for the future. Paul urges the Romans to offer their bodies and life as a living sacrifice, holy and pleasing to God.

The concept of sacrifice is relevant for any leader. Sometimes personal preferences have to be sacrificed when it is clear that the overall judgement of the team is to go in a different direction. There are times when a leader might have to offer themselves as a sacrifice when things have not gone as well as they should. If the overall boss is not happy about how a decision he has led on has played out then the right action is to face up to that responsibility and be clear that they are accountable for that decision. Offering to take the consequences can seem unnecessarily painful, but is often the best way of drawing a line under a particular issue and moving constructively forward into addressing the next phase.

There can be a risk of excessive vicariousness. When someone is always willing to take the blame others may seek to shift even more blame upon them in order to protect themselves. There is a proper balance between accepting responsibility as a leader and ensuring a proper review of what went wrong and where responsibility lay for different actions. Always offering yourself as a sacrifice is potentially as equally a dangerous distortion as hiding away from taking the consequences of actions that happened under your watch.

When you sacrifice a hope or aspiration as a leader it is worth observing yourself to check if you are expecting something in return. We can build up a sense of being owed something if sacrifices have an implied contractual intent. Sacrifices can, thereby, lead to resentment. It is well worth watching your own emotional reactions when you sacrifice a priority so you are not creating an unrealistic expectation on others which they may be entirely unaware of.

Jack felt badly let down by his boss. Jack had made a mistake but thought that he was acting consistently with the priorities of his boss. When the mistake came to light Jack's boss seemed only too willing for Jack to take the blame. Jack felt that he was sacrificing his own reputation to protect his boss from criticism.

Jack felt resentful that his boss showed no remorse for the inadequate steers he had given to Jack. Thankfully within a couple of weeks Jack's mistake had been largely forgotten. He was able to move on. Jack resolved that when he was in a leadership position he would not sacrifice a junior member of staff. Jack resolved that as a senior manager he would be accountable for the actions of his staff. This experience had been seared into his mind. He was clear that he would be deliberate in giving clear instructions when a task needed to be done and would be willing to take accountability if events flowed out in a way that had not been anticipated. He was not willing to sacrifice others for the greater good of either himself or the organization.

Jack knew he had to address the resentment he felt about his boss's decision not to defend him and sought to understand why his boss had responded in the way he did. Jack resolved to show mercy in the way he sought to understand the pressure upon his boss. Jack reached the point where he accepted what had happened and moved on from the touch of resentment about the approach of his boss.

For reflection

- Which of your personal hopes and aspirations do you need to sacrifice?
- How willing are you to sacrifice yourself for the sake of others?
- When you are sacrificial how do you ensure that you do not become resentful or frustrated?
- When are your sacrificial decisions genuine or when do they involve a degree of manipulation?

19

Community

A team that is working well brings a strong sense of shared community. There is a willingness to back each other up and pool resources and ideas. They know what the team is for and what can only be done by the team acting together. They are proactive in responding to a changing environment and build capability for sustainable change and maintain momentum as team members and move on.

Within an effective team there is a strong sense of community which is not frozen in time. There are moments of celebrating the past alongside a recognition that moving constructively into an unpredictable future is necessary. Team members recognize that they are part of interconnected communities with a need to build mutual understanding and a shared interest across the wider community.

The leader of any team is concerned about the wellbeing of its members and the wellbeing of the team as an organism. The team needs to live and breathe in a way that enables each part of the community to be supportive of each other, drawing on each other's strengths and allowing recovery time when different members of the team need the support of colleagues.

It is worth reflecting on when as a team member have you felt fully part of a team embracing shared values and behaviours? To what extent have you been working together to turn plans into reality? What has helped you feel part of that community so you have experienced support and have been able to engage in challenging dialogue when that has been necessary?

A theme within Genesis is the focus on God creating a community of people. At the start of Numbers the whole community of people are called together by Moses and Aaron. The strong sense of community is built upon at different points in Old Testament history. The rebuilding of the temple in Jerusalem under the leadership of Nehemiah is creating a new community drawing from the inspiration of the past. In building this new community the different trades people work together. During the day half the community worked on the rebuilding and the other half protected the city.

Jesus built a community around the disciples who came from very different types of work. Jesus encouraged them to work together and sent them out in pairs. He recognized that the degree of support for him was variable with Peter denying him and Judas betraying him. Jesus stretched their thinking into new ways of looking at the world. He washed his disciples' feet as a symbol of service to them. He equipped them to be ready to lead the embryonic Christian communities following his resurrection.

As a leader we are likely to be contributors to a number of different communities. There will be teams we lead, networks we engage with and other teams of which we are part. We will be part of a community of interacting interests and groups. The role we play can be destructive and divisive, or we can enable different parts of a wider community to understand each other and see the common good they are working towards.

The communities we lead can be messy. People are coming and going. There may be a variety of emotional reactions to situations with an ambivalence between people about whether goals and behaviours are genuinely shared. The challenge is understanding the messiness of communities and not being derailed by them. Progress comes from holding on to what is good and not allowing the imperfect to infect the sense of shared endeavour.

Sometimes the leader is called to lead from the front, crystallising a sense of direction while being sensitive to the needs and preferences of those within the organization. On other occasions the leader is serving the needs of those within a community by looking after their basic needs and interests. The metaphor of washing the feet of those working for, or with, you provides a visual image of service, and care and refreshing the hearts and minds of others.

You will continually be let down by those working for you. They may sometimes deny they have any responsibility. They might even try to undermine you and betray your interests. Surviving through this type of pressure requires a belief in what you are seeking to do and a willingness to accept the inevitability that things never run smoothly. If you accept that some people will let you down then the dominant emotion can be delight when they fulfil your hopes rather than dejection when they let you down.

Jack wanted to create the perfect team where there was clarity of direction, complementarities of contribution, and a strong commitment to each other's success. Jack selected people who he thought would want the team to succeed. When the project went through tough times and was being criticized there was a growing edginess in the team. People became annoyed with each other and frustration began to show. Jack knew he had to calm people down and reach a point where they rubbed along with each other accepting differences and not complaining about them.

Jack persuaded his team members that they should spend time

getting to know each others' hopes and preferences more. Jack invited them to share what gave them energy and what caused them frustration. He wanted to create a culture of openness and honesty, recognizing that there would always be underlying differences. His focus was on seeking to develop a sense of community where people would affirm each other and be willing to be challenged by each other. Jack wanted to develop a strong sense of people serving each other and looking after each other's needs when times were tough.

Jack encouraged team members to work in pairs or triads to develop ideas and joint plans. At the same time he created time for them as a team to share their learning with the intent of continually stretching their thinking about what might be possible going forward.

For reflection

- To what extent is a team you lead or are a member of part of a wider community of peoples?
- How do you handle the situation if a colleague denies you or betrays you?
- What does it mean to wash the feet of your colleagues?
- How best do you both serve and lead in a community of which you are part?

20

Communion

To what extent do you feel in communion with those people you work with? How important do you feel it is to have a sense of communion with your colleagues? Perhaps you do not want to feel too close a connection with those people you are working with. You want to keep your distance and protect your privacy. You want to be able to have good engagement and dialogue without infringing their or your privacy.

You are conscious that having a cup of coffee with someone can help create an informality that leads to a more conducive conversation. When sharing a meal with someone there is often a resulting ease in talking about both personal and work-related issues. Breaking bread together is a powerful metaphor about shared enterprise, engaging with related concerns and similar sources of nourishment. The giving and receiving of hospitality is part of a shared sense of communion and community. Restrictions on the giving of modest hospitality by organizations may be a proper response to the need for financial stringency but can be a false economy in terms of building constructive engagement and shared purpose.

The Passover feast is at the centre of Jewish celebration. The Communion service or the Eucharist is at the heart of the Christian tradition. The sharing of bread and the cup of wine are symbols of thankfulness, remembrance, and new life. Before the bread is broken and the cup shared there is a focus on thankfulness. The bread is described as the body of Christ given for others with the encouragement to eat and drink the elements in remembrance of the death and resurrection of Jesus.

The encouragement is to see engagement and equality coming from sharing bread and wine. Jesus talks of the greatest among you being like the youngest and the one who rules like the one who serves. The cup is described as the new covenant which is poured out for you. This symbolizes both the availability of the bread and wine and also the importance of the covenant relationship with future uncertainty being addressed together.

When you enter a new organization how do you build a sense of communion with others? Through learning about shared history and the hopes and dreams of the past you build a picture about the heritage of an organization you are entering. As you talk about hopes and dreams you are building an understanding of what gives the people within the organization purpose and hope. As you build a dialogue about emerging issues you are building a sense of communion and shared purpose together.

Communion involves sitting down together, listening to each other, sharing ideas and talking through possibilities. Communion includes hearing the perspectives of others, seeing different possibilities, touching into potential outcomes, tasting what might be possible and smelling out risks or potential adverse consequences.

How best do you build a sense of communion with people you have never met before? It might be about sharing a simple meal together. It will involve sitting around a shared table with good eye contact and listening. In the modern era it might be dialogue through Skype or Zoom with participants in different parts of the world.

Included within the communion service is the passing of the peace where a member of the congregation says to their neighbour, 'Peace be with you' with the response, 'And also with you'. This passing of the peace is intended to demonstrate that individuals are at peace with each other before they share communion. The handshake at the start of a meeting is akin to this type of passing of the peace. When I am facilitating a team event I often invite people to affirm each other's contribution and to say what they are going to most value about somebody's contribution going forward. This approach is seeking to replicate that sense of shared intent, both in terms of what is focused on and how team members work together.

Sonia did not feel comfortable working with a number of her colleagues. She kept her distance from them and was reluctant to engage in conversation. She had built up in her mind that some of her colleagues were always critical of her. She felt a victim of other people's prejudices. Part of her wanted to hold on to those prejudices as the resentment was a source of energy for her.

A couple of colleagues recognized the poisonousness of the situation. Sonia was damaging others and herself. There needed to be a breakthrough in her willingness to engage with others. These two friends had some long conversations with Sonia allowing her to explore her concerns and then encouraging her to see beyond those concerns into a potential future where there would be more openness and engagement. Sonia was persuaded to make overtures to the colleagues she had not spoken with recently. They were surprised by her suggestion of meeting for coffee and with some hesitation they agreed.

Gradually Sonia began to see that these colleagues were not critics, they were fellow travellers wanting to do their best and create a constructive atmosphere within the team. Sonia recognized that she had been too harsh on some of her colleagues and was willing to open her eyes to the possibility that they might be nice people.

The sense of sharing coffee together and talking through hopes and concerns helped move these tricky personal relationships into a different place. Sonia was beginning to allow herself to share her own story and be vulnerable. She was wanting to bring peace rather than discord into the working relationship: she knew she had to work at this and be consistent before she would be fully accepted, but she recognized that she was making some modest progress.

For reflection

- What particularly helps build a sense of communion with your colleagues?
- Who do you not feel in communion with and how best might you tackle that situation?
- What might 'sharing the peace' mean for you in a work situation?
- Who might it be appropriate to offer modest hospitality to and how might you use such occasions to build a sense of working together and shared hopes going forward?

21

Faithfulness

Faithfulness and loyalty have traditionally be seen as virtues in leaders and managers. Loyalty was rewarded through incremental pay. The good employee was expected to be faithful to the objectives and values of the organization for whom they worked.

What is important for a leader is not blind faith from those who work for them. What they need is a combination of committed faithfulness alongside a willingness to think creatively about how new problems can be addressed thoughtfully and constructively. Faithfulness is not about applying an age-old formula that may now be irrelevant. The fast pace of information technology means that the most appropriate ways to analyse and address issues are changing all the time.

Where faithfulness is important is in the application of standards, values and behaviours that are critical to an organization's success. Faithfulness to standards is about the quality of the product and ways of working. Faithfulness in terms of values and behaviours is about the way people are treated so that the vulnerable are safeguarded and the less confident are developed in a way that enables them to grow in confidence and effectiveness.

The dominant leader will expect their staff to be utterly faithful to them. That expectation will be fine in a crisis when urgent action is needed. But when there needs to be flexibility and freshness in thinking the expectation of blind faithfulness is a recipe for disappointment with its limitations on flexibility and adaptability.

Faithfulness is a strong theme in both the Old and New Testaments. The Psalms are full of visual references to faithfulness which springs forth from the earth or reaches into the skies. The faithfulness of the Lord is described as enduring for ever. Faithfulness is linked with righteousness. Isaiah describes faithfulness as a sash around the waist. In Proverbs love and faithfulness are linked together. The reader is encouraged to bind them round their neck and write them on the tablet of their heart.

Jesus talks of the faithful and wise servant. He commends some for their faith and comments on others about their little faith. He describes faith as starting as small as a mustard seed and then growing to become the tree. Jesus encourages those who have faith in him to be faithful to the truth. In his first epistle John talks of faith developing perseverance and encourages his hearers to be vigilant in being faithful to the truth.

When a group of individuals operate as a team they have to be faithful to the objectives of the team and faithful to their commitment to each other. For a team to be more than the sum of its parts it needs to depend on the energy and commitment that flows from individuals in a team being committed to each other's success.

Faithfulness in partnership with others is not about blind adherence to a set of rules. Dynamic faithfulness in a team depends on mutual understanding about the behaviours and ways of working. It includes a faithfulness to be frank and honest with each other and to not let colleagues down. Faithfulness to each other also involves flexibility in seeing where different team members can add value to each other and when there is the potential for the dynamic between the members to lead to a step-change in approaches to resolving difficult issues.

Faithfulness to be effective involves a constant recalibration of working relationships. In the religious setting an individual's faith is evolving in the light of their experience as their insights about people and situations continue to evolve. Similarly faithfulness in a work context cannot be static. Each individual's understanding of the world and the interplay between ideas and people needs to keep changing or it stagnates.

There are times when you lose faith in somebody because they have let you down. It is not in their interest or yours that you defend the indefensible. You will want to seek to understand and help somebody interpret what has happened to them, but faithfulness is never about protecting someone from facing up, over time, to reality.

Esther enjoyed working as the private secretary to a Government Minister and was utterly loyal to this Minister across the full range of her work. She understood his political philosophy and his preferences in terms of the way things were done. When the Minister was criticized her instinctive reaction was to defend him because she respected him and believed it was right to be faithful to him.

When a general election was held a new Government came into power and she was now working for a Minister from a different political party. She knew that she would have to switch her allegiance completely to the new Minister. She had been very loyal and faithful to the previous Minister and wondered how easy it would be to switch her loyalty.

What helped her work through this new situation was the recognition that she was being faithful to the principle of enabling the appointed Minister of the day to do their job effectively. The electorate had put a new political party in power. The requirement on Esther was to be faithful to that process and ensure she equipped the Minister to get up to speed quickly and build an effective working relationship with officials in the Government Department.

This experience was influential on Esther in her life outside work. She recognized that faithfulness is not about blind faith in one individual whatever they do. Faithfulness is more about being true to standards and behaviours that she applied in her interaction with different people in different spheres and phases of her life. Esther always wanted to act in good faith and be regarded as faithful and wise. She wanted to be faithful to the truth and to be able to say truth to power clearly in any situation. Faithfulness for Esther involved practical expressions of support and encouragement and setting high standards about behaviours and ways of working alongside respect for individuals

For reflection

- Have there been occasions when your loyalty and faithfulness to one individual has been too loyal and not taken account of changing circumstances?
- What for you does it mean to be faithful to the truth rather than faithful to an individual leader?
- How best do you switch your loyalties when you have a new boss who is very different to the previous boss?
- How do you express a faithfulness that is both committed and is detached enough to be objective?

22

Perseverance

Perseverance is about sticking at a task or intent over an extended period. Perseverance may have become engrained in us by our parents at an early stage. Our engagement with sport might have developed perseverance in us when the going gets tough. For me perseverance has developed through doing long walks in very different weathers. Perseverance on a wet and windy walk involves being properly equipped, knowing your destination, being single-minded as you move towards that destination and holding in your mind the delight of arriving safely when you are feeling battered and beaten by the wind and rain.

Sometimes perseverance means going slowly and treading carefully through boggy or rough terrain. On other occasions perseverance is about walking quickly down a predicted path. Perseverance can mean changing course when a path is blocked or a stream has flooded. There is then immense delight in reaching your destination exhausted and satisfied, glad to have been persistent even when you wondered how you would keep yourself going.

There will be moments in any job that are worthwhile when there are obstacles in the way. You may well not see a clear way through when there is little shared desire to reach a satisfactory conclusion. But with a clear goal and a few allies, plus a clear rationale and some affirmation, it is surprising what can be delivered, provided you keep your resolve and know how to retain your drive, and don't exhaust yourself too much.

Paul in his letter to the Romans linked perseverance and hope. He suggests that suffering because of faith in Jesus takes perseverance, perseverance leads to character and character leads to hope. In his letter to the Corinthians Paul described love as patient and kind: it does not delight in evil but rejoices with the truth. Love always protects, always trusts, always hopes and always perseveres. Paul talks of the way he sought to persevere in being an apostle. He commends the Thessalonians for their perseverance in handling persecutions and trials and encourages them to keep persevering through difficult situations.

In his letter to the dispersed churches James counts as blessed those who have persevered. He links perseverance to compassion and mercy. The book of Hebrews includes various references to faithfulness and perseverance. Moses is commended in Hebrews because he does not feel the king's anger and because he persevered. The writer of Hebrews encourages his readers to run with perseverance the race that is marked out before them surrounded by a great crowd of witnesses.

In a leadership role you are always surrounded by a crowd of witnesses. Some will be sceptics and might want you to fail. Others will be watching in order to learn from you. They are ready to acknowledge your perseverance and want some of that perseverance to rub off on them. You gain in confidence when through perseverance you are able to make a significant difference as a result of the work you are doing.

Perseverance has become more essential as a leader in the age of social media where everything you do is liable to be commented upon. Sometimes you will be showered in glory. On other occasions, unkind, unfair and hypercritical comments will accumulate on social media which need to be ignored if you are to keep up your focus and resolve.

It is important to know what enables you to have perseverance and what can sap perseverance. Perseverance will often flow from supportive working relationships, living your values and engaging with the tasks you are doing. The suffering that comes through painful hard work develops our perseverance which then feeds into our character, enabling us to be equipped to handle bigger challenges more effectively.

Perseverance is not about beating your head on a brick wall. Perseverance involves regularly reassessing whether the direction is right and what obstacles need to be addressed on the way. Perseverance often requires adaptability as there may be a different and better way to get to the outcome. Perseverance is not about staying rigid to one particular assumed best way of tackling an issue: it involves looking for a range of different means of getting to the desired outcome.

Mark felt that the charity where he worked was too set in its ways. They had a very hierarchical way of making decisions which was said to be justified by the need to be vigilant in using donors' money well. Mark felt that this rationale was used to justify criteria for the awarding of grants which were increasingly out of date when related to current needs. Mark felt worn down by the looks of disapproval from senior management when he suggested different ways of tackling issues, but he kept persevering.

The Chair of the charity asked Mark what he thought was the right way to tackle a particular issue and Mark felt uninhibited in expressing his views. The Chair began to play back some of those ideas to the Chief Executive without mentioning that they came from Mark. Mark was surprised and pleased to hear that the Chief Executive was suggesting some ways forward that Mark had already mentioned to the Chair. Mark did not gloat: he recognized that there are a range of different ways of being persistent and seeking to enable different people to understand possibilities for the future and to see the future through a new more positive lens.

Mark recognized that throughout his career he would need to be persistent if he was going to have the impact he wanted in whatever organization he worked. He recognized that he needed to be persistent in a way that sowed seeds in the minds of different people thereby allowing ideas to germinate and blossom at their own pace.

For reflection

- How far do you recognize in others that suffering produces perseverance, perseverance produces character and character produces hope?
- How best do you judge when you should persevere on the original course and when you should adapt your approach?
- When might you be at risk of blind perseverance, ignoring important changes in the context of requirements?
- How best do you recharge your batteries so that you can keep up your perseverance in tough times?

23

Kindness

We often remember words and acts of kindness far more readily than the detail of joint activities we are involved in. The kind and encouraging words when we are discouraged, or the act of kindness when we are in pain, can lift our spirits and remind us that pain can be transitory.

When someone is going through grief kindness is about being alongside them showing empathy and understanding. It is rarely about a deluge of words; it is about a quiet presence that enables someone not to feel isolated and alone.

Kindness flows when we are mindful about the emotions someone is going through. As we imagine what it is like to stand in their shoes we become sensitized to the type of pain they are feeling and what type of words can be a source of comfort and encouragement. The simple act of giving someone a cup of coffee or offering them a piece of fruit signifies a desire to engage and be supportive, with a simple act of kindness nudging someone into a shade more positive frame of mind.

Proverbs encapsulates human experience in suggesting that anxiety weighs down the heart but a kind word cheers it up. Proverbs describes the blessed as those who are kind to the needy. Proverbs suggests that one of the realities of kindness is that those who are kind benefit themselves but that the cruel bring ruin on themselves. When Daniel interprets the dream of Nebuchadnezzar he focuses on the message of being kind to the oppressed.

Luke records the encouragement of Jesus to love your enemies because God is kind to the ungrateful and wicked. The encouragement to be merciful is because God is merciful. The refrain of kindness occurs throughout the New Testament Epistles. Paul, when writing to the Corinthians, describes love as patient and kind. He encourages the Ephesians to be kind and compassionate to one another, forgiving one another. When writing to the Thessalonians Paul begins by acknowledging their kindness and encourages them to be kind to each other.

Kindness may seem an optional extra in a fast-moving world where business has to be transacted quickly. The expectation is that decisions are made rationally on the basis of the best possible evidence. Acts of support or kindness may be seen as a distraction which might mean the necessary objectivity for effective decision-making is obscured.

Taken to its extreme decision-making through rational, logical analysis leaves no room for emotional understanding or rapport. But most of us recognize that cold, clinical analysis can end in dispute and aggravation because data can always be interpreted in more than one way. What can break the logjam with competing and conflicting ways of viewing a problem is a sense of empathy and kindness that then results in protagonists beginning to understand why people take the view they do.

Simple acts of kindness can unlock conflict or defuse situations that can easily escalate into antipathy and even aggression. Kindness builds goodwill. It helps develop relationships where there can be give and take. Kindness at a very practical level can lead to an openness to think beyond one's own immediate fixed view when seeking a solution that wins acceptance. Kindness unlocks situations that have become fraught. Acts of kindness can take a difficult and uncomfortable relationship to another level with much more constructive engagement.

But even kindness has its limits. When you feel that your kindness is being taken advantage of, it is worth standing back and reflecting on what is happening. If you are being taken for granted and your kindness is assumed, it might be right to re-examine how your kindness is being received. In some situations, especially within a family or a community, there will be no preconditions about any limit on acts of kindness. The love within a family means that kindness continues however well or ungraciously it is received.

But in a work situation, and in many community situations, kindness needs to infuse the way individuals interact with each other so that it is two way. If the kindness is just one way resentment can build up if someone feels they have been taken advantage of.

It had been engrained in Francesca since she was a child that kindness was a necessary part of family and community life. Francesca had benefited from a community where kindness came naturally and was reciprocated. Her natural approach was to reach out with generosity and kindness to others which endeared her to many people. In her work as a manager in a supermarket Francesca's generous heart and practical kindness meant that people wanted to work for her. These acts of kindness generated a positive approach in her staff which meant that she built supportive and positive teams.

Just sometimes there would be employees who would take advantage of Francesca's kindness. They expected to have more flexibility in their working hours than others. They assumed that if they were late for work then Francesca's natural kindness would mean that they would not be reprimanded.

Francesca's boss recognized that her kindness was both a strength and a liability. The positive consequences were immense as people wanted to work for Francesca and were motivated by her inspirational approach, but it was painfully obvious that some people took advantage of Francesca's kindness with the result that there were rumblings from a number of staff that she needed to be stricter in applying fairness and not let kindness distort her perspective of what was involved in doing a job well.

Francesca persuaded herself that she should become tougher with the rationale that it was not helpful in the long run to let people subvert accepted norms and behaviours. Kindness in the long run was seeking to ensure her staff respected the discipline of the working arrangements and recognized the importance of fairness with consistent expectations being made of all the team members. Francesca gradually became tougher by being more deliberate in how she applied her natural kindness. There were always going to be moments when spontaneous kindness was important for Francesca, but she had also learnt to be more mindful of when her kindness was being taken advantage of, and when it was important to be deliberate in putting boundaries around that kindness.

For reflection

- In what situations does your kindness determine your actions?
- When might you be inclined to be rather more kind than ideally you should be with the result that some people might take advantage of your goodwill?
- What does it mean to be kind to the oppressed in a way that helps them move into a better place both physically and emotionally?
- How might you be one notch kinder and compassionate to your colleagues?

24

Patience

Is patience an asset or a liability? Patience is an essential prerequisite for any leader who is waiting for the moment to make a telling intervention. Patience can also be a liability if you end up waiting for something that is never going to happen. Patience can result in delaying a conversation that needs to take place. But impatience can mean that action is taken too quickly with counterproductive results.

You may be impatient for someone to retire so you can apply for their job. The best use of that period might be to further develop your credentials and experience so that when the job is advertised you are in a much stronger position than if it had been advertised at an earlier date.

Sometimes impatience can mean that our judgement becomes flawed. Our impatience leads to frustration or anxiety which can detrimentally affect our judgement. Our clarity of thinking can become blurred by the pressure we impose upon ourselves about the need for an early conclusion.

The pressure of expectation on us may lead us to push for early resolutions against our better judgement. The time to think through an issue from different angles may be squeezed out. We can become distraught with a sense of impotence that we have not been able to make more progress. Our patience becomes shorter and shorter. Handling our impatience may well mean seeking the views of trusted others and looking at a situation from a variety of different angles. It might involve walking away from a situation and trying to see it in a wider context.

Most of us remember people from our childhood who were immensely patient with us. They allowed us to grow up and test out different ideas, never losing their belief in us. We want to apply a similar level of patience with young people in our lives while desiring to steer them in the right direction.

In a work situation there can be moments when we might have too much patience. The working relationships in a team might be adequate but not good. We patiently observe the discord but decide not to intervene. But if we are too patient for too long we may lose the opportunity to seek to turn the culture in the team around. The words then spoken by people being critical of each other cannot be withdrawn. Sometimes the right thing to do is to act reasonably quickly to spot where problems might be developing and to take action, encouraging dialogue before the discord creates a situation that is much more difficult to redeem.

In the Old Testament patience is seen as a valuable virtue. The Psalmist talked about waiting patiently for the dawn. One of the most famous phrases from the Psalms is the encouragement to be still before the Lord and wait patiently. In Proverbs it is suggested that through patience a ruler can be persuaded and a gentle tongue can break a bone. Elsewhere in Proverbs is the assertion that a person's wisdom yields patience. In Ecclesiastes patience is described as better than pride.

Paul describes patience as one of the fruits of the Spirit. His hope for the Colossians is that they have endurance and patience. In Corinthians Paul talks about travails creating patience and kindness. James talks of how the farmer waits for the land to yield its valuable crops, waiting patiently for the autumn and spring rains. He uses this as a metaphor for being patient and standing firm. In Hebrews Abraham is described as having waited patiently. One of the themes in the book of Revelation is about patient endurance.

You may observe yourself saying through gritted teeth, 'I must be patient'. If you are trying hard to be patient, but the tone of the words and the look on your face is one of impatience, then the discomfort in your patience will be clear. It can be helpful to write down the reasons why you need to be patient and the risks if you are not patient. Doing this type of self-reflection can help calm your frustration down and allow the rational reasons to trump the emotional desire for quick action.

Sometimes it is a matter of suspending action, being patient and waiting to see what happens. We cannot control the next moves that people make. They may well need time to reach a decision and be comfortable in that decision. We cannot force them in a direction they do not want to go.

Patience may well involve walking away from situations for a period and focusing on another topic. It can mean seeking to view a contentious situation from a very different perspective, or seeking to see the benefits of no immediate decision.

On other occasions there is a need for virtuous impatience. When you see a situation that is stuck and people are embroiled in conflict there is a need for thoughtful impatience. This might mean ensuring that new evidence is properly considered, or seeking progress through getting the key protagonists in the room together and ensuring they talk to each other. You might need to hold a mirror up so that others see how their stalemate looks.

Sometimes you might be addressing impatience through very

direct and potentially provocative language. On other occasions you might be introducing a new piece of evidence or a question that enables people to reach their own conclusion that there is a stalemate which cannot go on forever.

Julia was getting increasingly fed up with her boss whom she regarded as indecisive. She kept wanting to say to her boss that his delay in making decisions was damaging morale within the organization. Julia's patience with her boss was being extremely tested. Julia also noticed that one of her staff seemed to be increasingly grumpy with her. When Julia asked why she was feeling grumpy this individual said that Julia was slow in making decisions and had not given her the steers to do her job well. It was a shock to Julia that she was being criticized for exactly the same reasons as she was critical of her boss.

Julia's first reaction was that her frustration with her boss was spilling into this relationship with her member of staff. Her second reaction was that she recognized that this member of staff was right and that Julia had not been clear enough about her expectations. Julia was letting her frustration with her boss contaminate the way she led her people. She didn't particularly want to have to make some decisions on key areas and was finding the indecisiveness of her boss an excellent excuse for her own indecisiveness.

Julia sought to understand why her boss was delaying certain decisions by asking him directly what the factors that he was focusing on were. It soon became clear to Julia that there were good reasons not to make a decision in the near future about some projects. Julia recognized that she could have been a bit more patient with her boss and not jump to conclusions that he was being a poor leader in not making decisions. This realization reminded Julia that she needed to be clear in explaining why she was making decisions and delaying others. Julia needed to be more patient with her boss but she also needed to give her staff enough explanation about the context and her reasoning so they were more willing to be patient with her.

For reflection

- Who do you observe combining well both patience and decisiveness? How do they balance those two skills well?
- Is the risk for you being too patient or too impatient and how do you correct for that?
- Where is your patience being tested at the moment and how best do you reach clarity in your own mind about how much patience is appropriate in this situation?
- In what current situations should you be more impatient and what action might you take?
- How might you deploy your patience in order to bring people with you more readily on a shared journey?

PART FOUR
Embodying Heart, Head and Hands

Being mindful of yourself and others involves engaging your heart, head and hands. It involves listening to your heart, engaging with your head and applying your hands. Mindfulness as a leader is about engaging with yourself and others in an open, honest and vulnerable way. Applying mindfulness includes being detached enough to see the world as it is, while being engaged enough to share the pain and joy of others.

There are many lenses through which mindfulness can be applied. Insights from Christian wisdom and perspective provide a way of looking at reality and applying mindfulness that is distinctive and complements approaches brought by others.

This section looks at how embodying the approaches or understandings that come from the Christian Gospel can help positively shape the attitude of mind we bring to leading others. The intent is to provide some brief, practical pointers about listening to our heart, engaging our head and applying our hands to enable constructive change to happen.

25

Heart

The mindful leader is listening with their heart as well as their ears. They are drawing on their heart to identify signs of new life and resurrection. Where events have not gone as well as people hoped, engaging with the heart brings a predilection to forgive, while recognizing the importance of an individual having the will to learn from experience. An attitude of love from a leader embraces care, compassion and constructive challenge, so that an individual can develop their potential to become the best version of themselves.

Bringing a sense of gentleness enables individuals and teams to listen to each other more carefully and treat each other with respect and deference. A focus on reconciliation can turn disenchantment or discord into stronger bonds based on shared, tough experiences.

Sharing our own vulnerability legitimizes others expressing their own vulnerability and engaging with how they draw insights from that vulnerability and turn it into a robust understanding of their own experience. Bringing a mind-set that there is hope to be found in any situation means there can always be a sense of possibility and moving on, however difficult a situation might currently feel. Looking for moments of joy in any situation, however tough, can lift the spirits and rekindle energy in a difficult situation.

The heart is at the centre of the physical body. These attitudes of the heart are central to how a mindful leader builds sustainability, commitment and continuous learning among the people they lead.

Potential questions that flow from embodying these themes might be:

- How might I encourage new life and resurrection in a situation where people are despondent and dejected?
- How might I articulate forgiveness to an individual to help enable them to learn from misjudgements and be able to move on?
- How might I more deliberately seek to show love and concern to those who cause irritation to me and others?
- Where might a greater degree of gentleness from me have a ripple effect prompting a gentler and more engaging approach to the way individuals engage with each other?
- Where might I be more deliberate in seeking to bring people into the room together and encourage constructive dialogue where there is a need for reconciliation?
- How might I show something of my own vulnerability and learning from tough situations and thereby encourage others to talk about their vulnerability and gain insights from others about how best to handle such situations?
- Where might I bring a sense of possibility and hope when individuals and teams are feeling bogged down by the realities they are addressing?
- Where might I encourage a sense of joy and expectation that is hopeful and not false?

My hope is that these questions allow you to apply insights from the heart that enable others to move forward in a constructive and concerted way.

26

Head

The mindful leader is applying insights from the head as well as the heart. The interplay of the rational and the emotional provides different ways of understanding issues and aspirations. If it is all heart there can be randomness and indecision. If it is all head decisions can appear cruel and inhumane.

When the mindful leader is using their brain they are focusing on what is the truth about the facts and perceptions in any situation. Getting to the unbridled reality in any situation, and being able to face up to the reality of this truth, is a key starting point for any leader.

There are moments when there needs to be a sense of crucifixion and death to mark a moving on and a leaving behind of attitudes and hopes that are inappropriate, dated or odious. A willingness to seek healing in yourself and others involves deliberate steps aimed at restoring harmony and allowing healing to create new strength rather than a continuous bleeding from old wounds.

Sustained healing comes through deliberate acts of rebuilding and the renewing of broken relationships alongside the lancing of deep-seated antipathy or resentment. Bringing humility means always being open to new ideas and approaches. Bringing freedom means you are not constrained by attitudes that flow from your cultural background or previous decisions.

Freedom involves the willingness to embrace change and see constructive possibilities in any situation. Applying judgement as a leader is about discernment and discrimination. It involves sifting the evidence and being willing to apply tough love. It includes speaking truth to power and not holding back from drawing attention to manipulation or abuse.

Bringing a sense of peace includes seeking to ensure that differences and discord are dealt with in a way that leads to a new equilibrium based on mutual understanding. Peace is not about perfect harmony, but it does involve mutual understanding and respect.

Applying self-control flows from bringing an understanding of the needs and preferences of the range of people you are engaged with as a leader, and setting clear priorities about how you use your time, energy and resources.

Examples of questions that it can be worth asking yourself might be:

- What is the truth in this situation that needs to be faced into?
- What attitude of mind needs to be left behind if there is to be a constructive move forward?
- Where can I encourage healing in attitudes and approaches, so that individuals and teams can move into a more constructive, forward-looking space?
- Where does my current situation require me to bring humility, both for my own good and for those looking to me for leadership?
- Where might I have more freedom to act than I had previously thought possible, and how best do I use that freedom?
- Where do I need to exercise clear judgement and explain my reasons carefully, even though I know this judgement will not be popular with everyone?

- How might I encourage a sense of peace and thoughtfulness where there is discord?
- In a busy and demanding situation what is the self-control I need to be exerting and encouraging in others?

Applying these questions allows us to bring a dispassionate object-ive assessment to help balance our emotional reactions. Allowing yourself to ask, 'what is my head saying?' alongside, 'what is my heart saying?' can provide two complementary perspectives that enable us to bring a considered mind-set to decisions.

27

Hands

Heart, head and hands are like a three-legged stool. The engagement of the heart needs to be complemented by consideration within the head. This joint endeavour then needs to be translated into actions of the hands.

Accepting responsibility to take action draws from the belief that it is possible to influence situations. Taking responsibility may involve sacrifice where your priorities are subjugated to the priorities of others. For any individual or team there will be times when hopes and aspirations have to be sacrificed for the greater good.

Working as part of a community means that many hands can be applied with your responsibility being less about what you do as an individual and more about how you enable a team or a wider community to have the desired impact. Communion is about how we engage together with colleagues, clients, customers and critics so that there is a mutual understanding and a hopefulness about a way forward.

Faithfulness involves clarity about loyalties and commitments, alongside a faithfulness to values and appropriate behaviours. Perseverance is key to making a difference and bringing determination to seek constructive change in situations you are involved in.

Kindness is at the heart of treating people as individuals and recognizing when they are in situations of need or vulnerability.

Patience flows from an understanding about timeliness and pacing, recognizing that individuals will be open to new ideas at different times prompted by changing circumstances and perceptions.

Potential questions to ask yourself might be:

- Where do I need to demonstrate that I accept full responsibility for next steps?
- What hopes do I need to sacrifice in order to be unencumbered moving forward?
- What might be my next steps in building a stronger sense of shared community with the people I engage with in my work?
- What practical steps might I take to create moments of shared communion within a team that is important to me?
- When faithfulness to a particular goal is being questioned, how best do I assess whether that faithfulness is well placed?
- In which areas do I need to renew my perseverance and how best might I do that?
- What acts of kindness that are important have I not been finding the space and time for?
- Where might I be exercising a greater degree of patience and why am I not doing so?

Your response to some of these questions might be to take action, while the response to others might be to deliberately hold back. Reflecting on these questions might enable you to practise more deliberately how you use your limited time and your mental and emotional energy.

My overall hope is that you reflect on the interplay of the insights from the heart, the promptings from the head, and the application of your hands. You will then be embodying insights that flow through the Christian Gospel, whatever your own personal philosophy.

There is a richness that flows from these twenty-four themes that can encourage and inspire leaders to be increasingly mindful about how they can win hearts and minds and join hands together for the common good.

Acknowledgements

The ideas in this book have been a long time in gestation. As undergraduate at Durham University I was grateful for prompting from Gerald Blake, a Professor in the Geography Department, about the interplay between a Christian perspective and political decisions. When I was at Regent College, Vancouver doing a Masters' Degree in Christian Studies in 1970–71 I was strongly influenced by Jim Houston, the first Principal at the College, about seeking to bring together Christian understanding into business and organizational life.

In my first career as a civil servant in the UK Government I learnt hugely from working with leaders shaped by many different philosophies. Working together in different teams enabled me to both understand the richness of other people's approaches and to seek to apply insights from a Christian understanding.

As a coach working with senior leaders in many different contexts and cultures my aim has been to enable them to be clear about their underlying values and how they influence the way they lead. I have encouraged individuals to draw from their religious and cultural traditions and appreciate how this provides a frame of reference within which they can operate as a sensitive and mindful leader.

I am grateful to Christine Smith at Canterbury Press who commissioned this book and has been very encouraging in turning my ideas into print. I am grateful to Rebecca Goldsmith and Lesley Staff for their practical contribution to generating the printed text.

The split of the book into the three sections of heart, head and hands came out of a conversation with Colin, my younger son, who always brings a very insightful approach to structuring ideas. I have had constructive dialogue with Ruth Ackroyd and Ruth Sinclair when developing ideas in the book. I am very grateful to both of them for the time they have given to reflect on these issues.

Jackie Tookey has typed the manuscript with her wonderful persistence and positive approach. Tracy Easthope has managed my diary with great skill to enable me to have some time to think and write.

My daughter, Ruth Roseblade, has been an immense help at a practical level in organizing my study and papers, and managing the despatch of books. My elder son, Graham Shaw, has embodied many of the characteristics set out in the book in the way he has led a church in Chester close to the university. My wife, Frances, has been a wonderful source of practical encouragement in the range of activities I have been involved in.

I am particularly grateful to those colleagues at Regent College, Vancouver who have continued to encourage me in the thinking, writing and teaching about what it means to be a mindful leader at a time of rapid change and high expectations. Jeff Greenman as President of the College has been a consistent and positive supporter and encourager for which I am immensely grateful.

I have always felt supported by David Wilkinson, the Principal of St. John's College Durham where I was a Council member for many years. I have dedicated this book to Jeff Greenman and David Wilkinson as they are exemplars of mindful, caring and decisive leadership through demanding times.

I am grateful to Ian Kenyon who has written the foreword to the book. Ian has brought an incisive and level-headed approach to senior leadership roles in the private, voluntary and public sectors. He has been a source of sound advice to many individuals and teams drawing on his experience and his Christian perspective.

I am delighted that Justin Welby, the Archbishop of Canterbury, has endorsed the book. When I was the Government Regional Director for the North East of England in the early 1990s Justin Welby was a student at Cranmer Hall and lived a few doors up the road from us. It was clear then that he would bring a lot of practical wisdom into future leadership roles.

Books and Booklets by Peter Shaw

Mirroring Jesus as Leader. Cambridge: Grove, 2004.

Conversation Matters: how to engage effectively with one another. London: Continuum, 2005.

The Four Vs of Leadership: vision, values, value-added, and vitality. Chichester: Capstone, 2006.

Finding Your Future: the second time around. London: Darton, Longman and Todd, 2006.

Business Coaching: achieving practical results through effective engagement. Chichester: Capstone, 2007 (co-authored with Robin Linnecar).

Making Difficult Decisions: how to be decisive and get the business done. Chichester: Capstone, 2008.

Deciding Well: a Christian perspective on making decisions as a leader. Vancouver: Regent College Publishing, 2009.

Raise Your Game: how to succeed at work. Chichester: Capstone, 2009.

Effective Christian Leaders in the Global Workplace. Colorado Springs: Authentic/Paternoster, 2010.

Defining Moments: navigating through business and organisational life. Basingstoke: Palgrave/Macmillan, 2010.

The Reflective Leader: standing still to move forward. Norwich: Canterbury Press, 2011 (co-authored with Alan Smith).

Thriving in Your Work: how to be motivated and do well in

challenging times. London: Marshall Cavendish, 2011.

Getting the Balance Right: leading and managing well. London: Marshall Cavendish, 2013.

Leading in Demanding Times. Cambridge: Grove, 2013 (co-authored with Graham Shaw).

The Emerging Leader: stepping up in leadership. Norwich: Canterbury Press, 2013, (co-authored with Colin Shaw).

100 Great Personal Impact Ideas. London: Marshall Cavendish, 2013.

100 Great Coaching Ideas. London: Marshall Cavendish 2014.

Celebrating Your Senses. Delhi: ISPCK, 2014.

Sustaining Leadership: renewing your strength and sparkle. Norwich: Canterbury Press, 2014.

100 Great Team Effectiveness Ideas. London: Marshall Cavendish, 2015.

Wake Up and Dream: stepping into your future. Norwich: Canterbury Press, 2015.

100 Great Building Success Ideas. London: Marshall Cavendish, 2016.

The Reluctant Leader: coming out of the shadows. Norwich: Canterbury Press, 2016 (co-authored with Hilary Douglas).

100 Great Leading Well Ideas. London: Marshall Cavendish, 2016.

Living with Never-ending Expectations. Vancouver: Regent College Publishing 2017 (co-authored with Graham Shaw).

100 Great Handling Rapid Change Ideas. London: Marshall Cavendish, 2018.

The Mindful Leader: embodying Christian wisdom. Norwich: Canterbury Press, 2018.

Forthcoming Books

100 Great Leading Through Frustration Ideas. London: Marshall Cavendish, 2019.

Leadership to the Limits: freedom and responsibility. Norwich: Canterbury Press, 2019.

Booklets

Riding the Rapids. London: Praesta, 2008 (co-authored with Jane Stephens).

Seizing the Future. London: Praesta, 2010 (co-authored with Robin Hindle-Fisher).

Living Leadership: finding equilibrium, London: Praesta, 2011.

The Age of Agility. London: Praesta, 2012 (co-authored with Steve Wigzell).

Knowing the Score: what we can learn from music and musicians. London: Praesta, 2016 (co-authored with Ken Thompson).

The Resilient Team. London: Praesta 2017 (co-authored with Hilary Douglas).

Job Sharing: a model for the future workplace? London: Praesta 2018 (co-authored with Hilary Douglas).

Copies of the booklets above can be downloaded from the Praesta website (www.praesta.co.uk).

About the Author

Peter Shaw has coached individuals, senior teams and groups across six continents. He is a Visiting Professor of Leadership Development at Newcastle, Chester and De Montfort Universities, and is a Professorial Fellow at St John's College, Durham University. He has been a member of the Visiting Professorial Faculty at Regent College, Vancouver, since 2008. He has written 27 books on aspects of leadership: some are translated in seven different languages.

Peter's first career was in the UK Government where he worked in five Government Departments and held three Director General posts. Peter has been a member of governing bodies in higher and further education. He is a licensed lay minister (Reader) in the Anglican Church and plays an active role in the Church of England at parish, diocesan and national levels. He is a Lay Canon of Guildford Cathedral and Chair of Guildford Cathedral Council.

Peter holds a doctorate in Leadership Development from Chester University. He was awarded an honorary doctorate at Durham University for 'outstanding service to public life', and an honorary doctorate by Huddersfield University for his contribution to leadership and management.

In his coaching work Peter draws from his wide experience both as a leader and as a coach to leaders in many different contexts. He seeks to bring insights into his coaching work with individuals and teams which are underpinned by his Christian faith and understanding. His focus is about enabling individuals and teams to step up in their effectiveness so that they have a clear vision about what they are seeking to do, apply the values that are most important to them, know how to bring a distinctive value added and recognize their sources of vitality.

Peter finds time to reflect when on long distance walks of which he has done thirty. Recent ones include the Machu Picchu trail, the Lady Anne Way, the Weardale Way, the Cotswolds Way, the Peak District Limestone Way, the Nidderdale Way, and the North Yorkshire Moors Inn Way.